CREATIVE THOUGHT REMEDIES

Alex Jones

DeVorss & Company
P. O. Box 550, Marina del Rey, CA 90294-0550

Copyright © 1986
by Alex Jones

All rights in this book are reserved. Except for quotations in book reviews, no part of this book may be reproduced in any form without written permission from the author.

ISBN: 0-87516-566-4
Library of Congress Catalog Card Number: 85-73847

Third Printing, 1989

Printed in the United States of America

Dedication

This book is humbly dedicated to all as an instrument to uplift consciousness on the wings of Self-Realization.

With special thanks to Ann Emerson for her editorial work.

When man begins to look at himself as he is,
then his work has finally begun.

When man looks at himself and others and sees
only Spirit, then his work is done.

Contents

Preface

Introduction

Part One: Understanding the Workings of Consciousness

Freedom of Choice
(page 3)

Understanding the origin of life-promoting and life-diminishing processes. Perceiving the forces and attitudes that keep us in delusion and Spirit's method of taking us out of the clutches of ignorance.
Realizing how our conscience operates and its effect upon us.

The Contrast between Life-Promoting and Life-Diminishing Actions
(page 8)

A look at the positive qualities that lead to happiness and those that lead to misery.

Winning As a Way of Life
(page 11)

Attitudes needed to overcome destructive habits.

Influences on Behaviour
(page 15)

Understanding internal and external influences.

Choosing What We Want to Become
(page 19)

How thoughts and feelings form habits that determine our personalities.

Disturbing Thoughts and Emotions
(page 23)

Comprehending the problems caused by negative emotions.

Part Two: What Promotes and What Diminishes Joyous Living

Self-Deprecation or Self-Confidence
(page 29)

An overview of self-defeating and self-enriching attitudes.

Desires
(page 32)

Observation of desires that benefit us and those that limit us.

Creative Attitudes
(page 36)

Discerning the positive aspects of fear and letting go of negative fears.

Master or Victim
(page 42)

Dealing with situations in life from a state of control rather than slavery.

Healing Wisdom
(page 45)

Attitudes that make it possible to deal constructively with anger.

Joyousness or Moodiness
(page 50)

Transforming moods into positive experiences of optimism.

Calmness or Restlessness
(page 53)

Learning the attitudes necessary to become calm instead of restless or agitated.

Gossip, Judgment, and Criticism
(page 57)

An overview of gossip and how to escape its destructive net.

Jealousy and Envy
(page 61)

Learning the difference between destructive jealousy and constructive envy.

Flattery and Criticism
(page 65)

Inner understanding to use in meeting flattery and criticism.

Part Three: Virtues

Self-Love
(page 71)

Learning to love as our Creator loves us.

Success Pointers
(page 74)

Learning the rules for successful living.

Lasting Happiness
(page 78)

Learning the ability to be happy materially, mentally, and spiritually.

Part Four: Relationships

Relationships
(page 89)

The basic elements of relationships.

A Happy Relationship
(page 93)

Attitudes necessary for a happy relationship.

Elements Harmful to a Relationship.
(page 95)

Guidelines for creative, enriching relationships.

Part Five: Behaviour Skills

Be Your Real Self
(page 99)

Analyzing your freedom to express your true personality instead of being controlled by society, custom, and other people's expectations.

Psychological Conflict
(page 102)

Understanding the inner conflicts one has when trying to overcome life-quenching habits.

Guilt
(page 107)

Attitudes dealing with mistakes and regrets.

Inner Voices on Food
(page 111)

Awareness of the thoughts that arise when learning self-regulation.

The Healing Crisis
(page 115)

Light on what happens when we receive spiritual healing or healing through natural means.

Part Six: Personalized Thought Remedy Chart

Making and Using a Personal Chart
(page 121)

Learning who and what you are and can become.

Preface

Many books have been written on spiritual, mental, and physical attitudes to uplift mankind and make us realize that we are children of light. Jesus answered them, "Is it not written in your law, I said, Ye are gods?"* "I have said, Ye are gods; and all of you are children of the most High."† Truth is timeless and in essence simple. Very often in one's busy life, there just is not much time to sit down and study the scriptures. When we do make the effort to study them and other helpful writings, there always seems to be so much to try to keep in mind. When we come back to study them at a later date, we may feel that we must start again at the beginning. At times we read an inspiring statement and feel its truth, then forget it, and when we go back to find it we realize that it is now lost in many pages of print.

The guidance presented in this book is taken from timeless wisdom of the ages and condensed in an easy-to-understand visual form. By reading and studying each Thought Remedy Chart and its corresponding introduction, the healing essences can register in your consciousness and help you to correct unstable attitudes that cause unhappiness and illness. After you have studied the charts, each one can then act as a quick reference point to glance at when necessary to gain its inspiration. Whatever chart is found to be particularly helpful during a period in your life could be placed where you can look at it as a quick guide. This is also valuable to do as you work on and complete your own personalized Thought Remedy Chart at the end of the book. A glance at, and recognition of, its truth could save you untold misery and bring you peace and happiness.

*John 10:34
†Psalms 82:6

Introduction

Mankind is in essence pure consciousness, but we have accepted the idea that we have conscious and subconscious minds only. When our life energies flow outward and contact the world of sense perceptions and muscular activity, then we are playing in our conscious mind. Our organs of sight, smell, taste, touch, and hearing receive impressions from the outside world, and these travel along the sensory nerves to the brain, where perceptions are organized into conceptions and thoughts.

When we are dwelling in the realm of memory and imagination, then we have contacted the subconscious mind. We also explore the subconscious during our sleeping and dreaming states when the life energy is completely shut off from the sensory world. Wherever our energy is determines what state of consciousness we are in. When the energy flows outward, we are in the conscious state; and as the energy moves inward towards the spine and brain, we experience other states of consciousness.

The superconscious mind is beyond sense perceptions, thoughts, memory, imagination, and dreams. In this state of consciousness the energy is concentrated at the pineal gland or spiritual eye and the medulla oblongata. When we are in touch with the superconscious mind, we are in touch with our souls, and it is here that the presence of God will be felt. We begin to come in contact with this realm when our minds are completely still. "Be still and know that I am God."*

As a pond reflects the moon when it is calm, so when our minds are calm we will reflect the presence of God within. When God's presence is awakened within us we will feel love, peace, joy, wisdom, power, bliss, and so on. The sixth sense of intuition will be awakened within, and we will be in tune with the mind of God. In deep sleep, when we pass beyond the land of dreams, we enter into the paradise of our superconscious minds.

We all have an inkling of having reached this state when, upon awakening, we feel refreshed, energized, and joyous. Most of us have glimpsed this blessed state at one time or another. Very often when we are half asleep and half awake we feel a great joy and peace bubbling up from within. We have stumbled into the perimeter of the superconscious mind. Meditation is the art of traveling to this celestial place consciously and at will.

If we continue our meditative journey further within, we will come in touch with Christ Consciousness. Everything in this world is subject to change, but God is changeless. God is in everything and everything is in God. The Changeless Spirit that dwells in every atom of a changing world is known as the Christ Intelligence or Christ Consciousness state. Jesus,

* Psalms 46:10

through self-discipline and meditation, expanded His consciousness and was aware of the entire universe as His own body. He found that He became one with the changeless God in every atom of creation.

Put a drop of dye in a glass of water and what happens? It spreads and is found in every particle of the water. In the same way, when we begin to tune in to the Holy Ghost or Eternal Spirit in meditation and hear the sacred Word we begin to expand in that holy vibration everywhere. Our heritage is omnipresent, and as we come in contact with the Christ Consciousness state, we begin to realize that our bodies are the universe, even as Christ did.

God the Father, beyond the vibrations of creation, is known as Cosmic Consciousness. He is the Supreme Intelligence that has created all other vibrations or states of consciousness. Everything in the cosmos is made up of different rates of vibration, consciousness, or energy and has been created by the Infinite Mind of God. The Great Spirit is dreaming the play of creation in His mind. When we awaken from the dream of life we will realize that we are one with the Divine Dreamer and say, "I and my Father are one."† We are made in the image of God, and through the workings of evolution, we are all trying to get back to our eternal home, Cosmic Consciousness.

We have all descended from God through the different levels of consciousness, and we must retrace our footsteps to go back to Him. Our Cosmic Consciousness state is buried within us and is like a diamond that is ready to reflect all the knowledge and love of the Supreme Giver. We have, however, covered our diamond consciousness with the mud of worldly concerns through incarnations of interaction with the physical world of sensations. We have set up these worldly tendencies in our conscious and subconscious minds which are like ripples on the lake of the soul preventing us from experiencing our Godlike nature. Some of these worldly patterns are unique to each of us and some are universal to all mankind.

Through interactions with certain types of people and situations, we have developed deep grooves of mental and emotional responses that are instantaneous and automatic. Many people are not aware that they are living robot-like, responding to situations from a pattern that they set up years ago.

Almost every disease of mankind is a result of negative thinking, feeling, and acting. By dwelling on negative emotions we trigger physical reactions that use up our vital energies and lower the body's vitality and so weaken our resistance to all types of diseases —physical, mental, and spiritual. If we hold hatred in our hearts for anyone, we will pollute our consciousness with that hatred. In time the hatred and resentment will overwhelm and affect the heart, which is the seat of love.

Our consciousness is like a container and holds whatever we decide to put into it, both life-promoting and life-diminishing impulses. As children of God we have the gift of free will and choice and can bring into consciousness or remove from it whatever we choose. Very often, however, our will is paralyzed by tendencies that are the result of our early conditioning or other incarnations.

† John 10:30

We usually are quite unaware of all these invisible influences and wonder why whenever we are in certain situations these responses manifest themselves. At times there is no rhyme or reason to why we behave the way we do. The answer lies in the fact that we have created these automatic responses sometime, somewhere in the past. If we think back over our youth and reflect on our predominant personality traits, then we can begin to have some insight into some of our characteristics.

If you sincerely want to change, this book can help you to become aware of the universal patterns of mankind in which we are all caught, and to discover your own unique patterns. By bringing yourself in touch with these patterns, you can understand them and see how they affect your life. As you become more and more aware, you will be able to control these patterns and no longer be a puppet to their influences. You will come to see how you can improve your relationships with other people by removing the patterns that have resulted in breakdowns in communication and understanding.

In addition, this book outlines the spiritual tendencies or patterns that will bring you back in touch with your soul. By retraining your thoughts and emotions you can become master of yourself, and the light of your soul will again be able to shine forth. You will find that as your soul qualities blossom, your relationships with people will function on a much higher plane and be more fulfilling and rewarding. By following the instructions in this book you can build a firm and solid foundation in the spiritual life, so that you will be steadfast and secure as you expand your consciousness through meditation to Cosmic Consciousness.

Each section and condensed chart that follows is a thought remedy. Study these remedies and the affirmations thoroughly and adapt and relate them to your own life. Think about how they apply to you, and see if you can recognize something of yourself in each topic covered. By doing so you will have a deeper understanding of human behaviour and of your own. These thought remedies and affirmations are an invaluable aid in your own self-analysis, and in this system they prepare you for the final section of the book—your own personalized Thought Remedy Charts. These charts can be a revelation to you in helping you discover all your own unique patterns and interactions with others.

Part One

UNDERSTANDING THE WORKINGS OF CONSCIOUSNESS

We Are Whatever We Entertain
In Our Consciousness.

Freedom of Choice

Laws of Life

The One Spirit has created the universe out of vibration. From one pure beam of Light other vibrations arose: all natural forces, thoughts, feelings, and everything that is solid, liquid, fire, gas, and ether.

In essence Supreme Intelligence created everything out of Itself, but God is also beyond vibration. When a soul at last becomes one with the Divine it realizes its true nature of oneness with all that is. Unless a soul or entity has attained to Cosmic Consciousness it is subject to the laws of creation—or the law of opposites. What this means is that a soul feels separation from Spirit and is under the influence of vibrations both harmonious and inharmonious, and aware of duality.

Harmonious, refined vibrations are closer to the Creator. Inharmonious grosser vibrations are the creation of a delusive intelligent cosmic force known in Christianity as Satan and termed *Maya* in Eastern thought and philosophy. If a soul is preoccupied with grosser, inharmonious vibrations, then it will be unable to perceive the refined intelligence of Spirit behind that vibration. If a soul chooses harmonious vibrations, then it will feel a greater affinity with the Source of all life.

Free Will

Spirit has created all of us with free will. Not only can we choose between harmonious or inharmonious vibrations; we can create them as well. We are made in the image of God and can create peace and beauty, as many of the masters have done, or chaos and destruction, as Satan or Maya does.

With freedom of choice we can choose or create light or shadow, love or hate, peace or agitation, joy or sorrow. If we accept and manifest love over hate, peace over restlessness, inner perceptions over body consciousness, we are drawn closer to our divine nature. If we turn our will and action in the opposite direction, we will be drawn deeper into delusion and suffering.

If our focus of attention is solely on denser vibrations, then we will perceive matter only.

By concentrating on matter we will ultimately expect pleasure from it and in turn have endless desires for material objects and endless disappointments. By feeling fleeting glimpses of happiness from sense pleasures, we become attached to them. Attachment in turn leads to feelings of possessiveness and overindulgence. From these spring the inharmonies of frustration, dissappointment, greed, violence, and disgust.

Conflict in the Mind

We are floating on the sea of creation and deciding within ourselves which vibrational tendencies to choose. Through trial and error we each eventually learn that choosing inharmonious vibrations, no matter how tempting, results in disappointment, emptiness, and sorrow. If we listen to our inner prompting and discriminating feelings, we begin to realize that certain desires and actions can lead to lasting soul happiness. Through uplifting thoughts, feelings, and actions that serve and help mankind we soon begin to discern uplifting, satisfying, harmonious vibrations within ourselves. The spiritual qualities of love, peace, empathy, and compassion unfold from within and bring contentment. We realize a greater sense of being by developing and manifesting these qualities than through pursuing outward attachments.

Inner Perceptions

The person who finds satisfaction in inner perceptions will ultimately seek methods of going deeper within, usually through prayer and meditation. By stilling the restless body and mind other states of consciousness begin to unfold, and the perceptions of Spirit are felt.

Once the presence of God is experienced or intuitively realized, then love for God is born. Love is the magnet that draws the soul to God and God to that soul. The more the soul loves, the greater is the perception of the Creator's Love. In ever-increasing love the soul can reach its highest fulfillment—oneness with Spirit.

Chart Study: Freedom of Choice

Our first summary chart depicts the pattern of creation. The main idea in studying the following charts is to determine how we personally relate or fit into them. Through introspection we can discover at which stage we presently are and decide upon the best method of advancement. You will note in the charts that the positive, uplifting qualities are indicated on the right and the limiting ones on the left.

You are invited to analyze your life and determine in which direction you are now going and to decide in what direction you prefer to travel. If you, the reader, have decided that it is to your advantage to remove limiting habits and to evolve Godward, then please proceed to our following exercise.

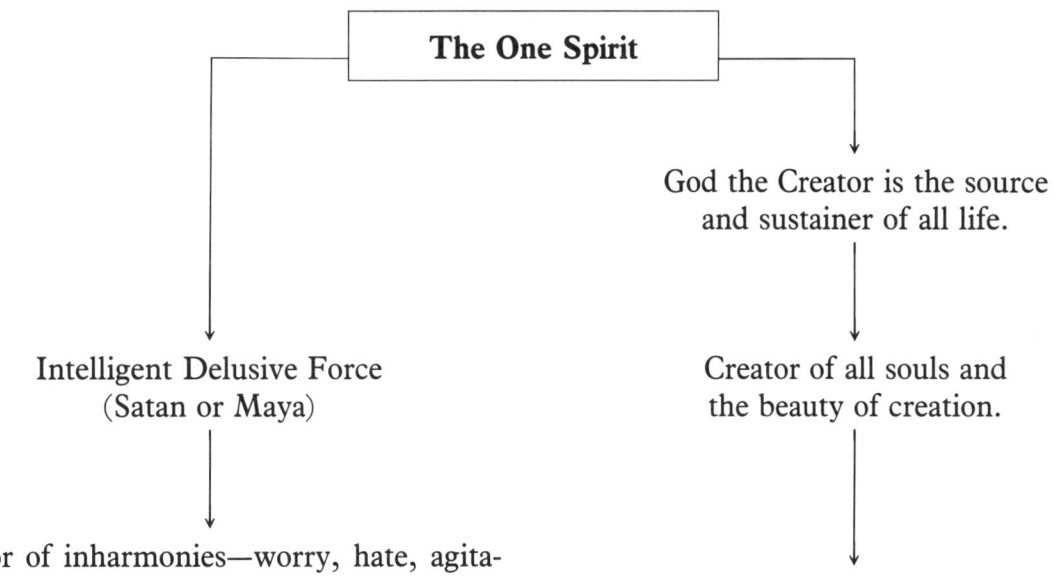

FREEDOM OF CHOICE

The One Spirit

God the Creator is the source and sustainer of all life.

Creator of all souls and the beauty of creation.

Creator of the harmonies of love, peace, joy, compassion, patience, confidence, self-knowing, etc.

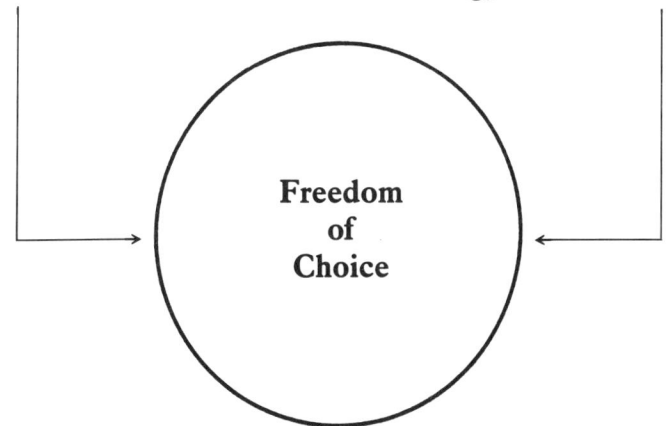

Intelligent Delusive Force (Satan or Maya)

Creator of inharmonies—worry, hate, agitation, misery, sorrow, indifference, pride, inferiority feelings, greed, envy, anger, resentment, etc.

Freedom of Choice

FREEDOM OF CHOICE

The One Spirit

Intelligent Cosmic Delusive Force (Satan or Maya)

The Creative Spirit gave Maya independent power to maintain the universe and bestow on each soul a feeling of separation from its infinite source that it might manifest its own individuality.

↓

Maya misused this power and created patterns of disharmony in direct opposition to Spirit's patterns of harmony.

↓

Maya caused mankind to see only matter and to lose awareness of Spirit.

↓

Through contact with matter mankind created desires for material objects and began to focus on the temporary pleasures of the senses.

↓

Through continuous contact with the senses mankind became attached to material pleasures.

↓

Attachment led to overindulgence. From overindulgence there arose greed, fear, anger, and hatred, and mankind lost the memory of its connection with God.

↓

Acting against Our Birthright

Divine Magnetic Attractive Force of Love

Love is drawing all souls to unite in oneness in the bosom of Spirit.

↑

Love is stronger than any of Maya's tests, and by unfolding in love and following the patterns of Spirit, all souls may purify themselves and realize their oneness with God.

↑

Meditation and prayer awaken inner soul qualities and God's love for us and our love for God.

↑

Meditation and prayer awaken the all-knowing power of intuition, which aids the discriminative feelings that show us where our true happiness lies.

↑

When man listens to the discriminative feelings of inner knowing he begins to employ his will and motivation to turn his attention away from material desires and toward God and serving mankind.

↑

Listening to the Inner Voice of Spirit

Battleground of the Mind

| Whenever we follow the patterns of Maya we are pushed deeper into delusion. | Each soul is made in the Image of God and, like Spirit, has free will and free choice to bring into its consciousness whatever it chooses. | Whenever we follow the patterns of Spirit we are drawn closer to God and our ultimate good. |

AFFIRMATIONS

Affirmations are positive statements about something we want in our lives. When we focus our "whole" attention on them, knowing their rightness for us and visualizing and feeling as if they were true for us, we reach that important part of ourselves. If we persist, we can then reprogram ourselves and so bring the desired attribute, situation, or attitude into our lives and automatic reactions.

The affirmations in this book are intended for this purpose. After each section and each Creative Thought Remedy Chart there are listed a number of suggested affirmations. Choose one that fits what you want in your life, or use them as guidelines to create your own. It is necessary to work with them persistently if you want to replace the old way of reacting or being. Remember that it took you a long time to build up the patterns that now control or direct you. It is suggested that an affirmation, once undertaken, should be written and repeated aloud ten times a day (twice a day is better) for at least three weeks or 21 days in order to establish it firmly. Individual times will vary according both to how deeply entrenched a habit or mode of response is and to your own flexibility. See chapter "Winning As a Way of Life" for a more detailed discussion on the practice of affirmations.

SUGGESTED AFFIRMATIONS

**I am a free-born son/daughter of God.
The power of choice is mine.
I choose to seek my own inner guidance
And link my life with my highest good.**

**Life is a journey I am taking;
I can choose which way I will go.
I am attuning to the Divine Plan
And making choices that benefit me and mankind.**

**I am using my God-given power of choice
To take charge of my life and make it what I want it to be.**

The Contrast between Life-Promoting and Life-Diminishing Actions

To Transform an Inharmonious Quality, Concentrate on the Opposite Harmonious Quality

Observe and determine which thoughts and feelings you are manifesting. Eliminate destructive, disturbing ones and develop uplifting ones that rejuvenate and bring lasting peace and happiness. The most effective way to remove a life-diminishing habit is to concentrate on the opposite—a life-promoting habit. If you have trouble with anger, then it is effective to concentrate on the opposite quality of calm and peaceful understanding. If sorrow is clouding your consciousness, then concentrate on happiness. If greed manifests and rules your life, then practice unselfishness and generosity, and so on.

If you feel you have no life-diminishing habits, then work on the life-promoting qualities that you feel an affinity with. Concentrate on and practice these until you own and become one with their quality and come to know the presence of their Spirit.

Chart Study: The Pull between Life-Promoting and Life-Diminishing Actions

In our next chart we take a more extensive look at what is harmonious and what is not. Here we again see that consciousness, having free will, has the option between life-promoting and life-diminishing actions.

THE CONTRAST BETWEEN LIFE-PROMOTING AND LIFE-DIMINISHING ACTIONS

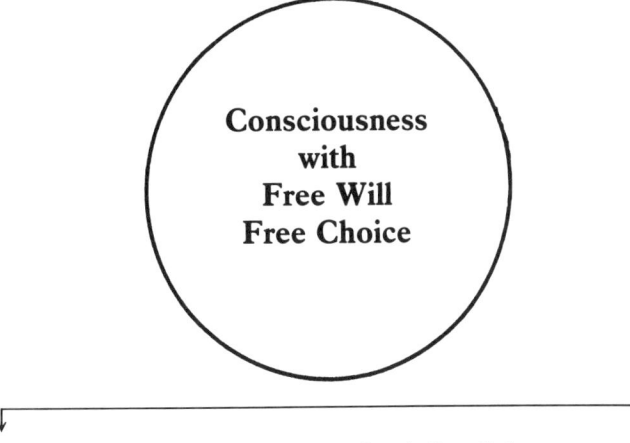

Consciousness with Free Will Free Choice

↓

Ego consciousness
(body-bound soul, restless mind)

↓

Physical Sense Pleasures
(desires and attachments to sensations)

↓

Crooked Mental Tendencies

↓

Driving ambition, anger, jealousy, unkindness, disharmony, greed, hatred, harshness of thought/word/deed, selfishness, cruel actions, bitterness, sense attachments, meanness, fear, resentment, worry, blaspheming, quarrelsomeness, sex abuse, overeating, pretending goodness, covetousness, high-handedness, laziness, timidity, spiritual indifference, weakness of will, moodiness, depression, ignorance, cruelty, immorality, gossiping, impatience, superiority or inferiority complexes, nervousness, urge to hurt, desire to kill, betrayal, deceit, unscrupulousness.

↓

Sickness, worries, unhappiness, spiritual emptiness, dissatisfaction, disillusionment, depression and despair.

↓

Soul Qualities
Awareness of oneness as our true nature, discrimination, self-confidence, meditative calmness and peacefulness, responsibility for self, intuition and inner knowing, kinship with all life.

↓

Inner Divine Qualities

↓

Love, peace, joy, spiritual power, wisdom, sincerity, compassion, humility, kindness, balance, courage, loyalty, unselfishness, fearlessness, sweetness, morality, courtesy, firmness, justness, honesty, congeniality, aestheticism, joy in meditation.

↓

Self-Realization.

SUGGESTED AFFIRMATIONS

>I yearn to be joyous and at peace,
>Feeling the fullness of love in my heart.
>I now choose to express
>The inner divine qualities of my soul.
>
>I focus on what promotes my well-being and leave behind
>what does not serve my best good.
>
>I know life is a series of choices;
>On one side is truth and on the other delusion.
>I am moving closer to the Light of Truth;
>I now choose that which uplifts me and makes me whole.
>
>I am drawing to me all that is of beauty, harmony, joy,
>wholeness, love, and balance.

Winning As a Way of Life

Meditation and Affirmations

Meditation and affirmations are two methods that work hand-in-hand to help a soul attain the transforming attitudes necessary to rise above limiting habits and develop life-promoting ones. Through meditation we can attain a state of stillness beyond mental and emotional restlessness. In this state we spontaneously begin to become aware of the inner divine soul qualities and manifest them outwardly. If you sincerely use a program of meditation, then you can begin realizing your highest potential.

Affirmations

The main focus of this book is to teach introspection and the use of affirmations that can change your life. Affirmations are statements of truth or positive, motivating thoughts. By repeating these, your inner self learns to concentrate on and accept these new, more effective patterns.

Affirmations work on the principle of magnetism. When we focus our concentration on a thought, a force field is set up drawing within its circle that which is being affirmed. This can work negatively as well as positively, so it is very important to concentrate only on what is uplifting and empowering.

Affirmations and Concentration

When affirming for a particular result, we must free ourselves from all that is destructive or negative. If you repeat positive affirmations but hold disturbing or negative beliefs, thoughts, and feelings, then you will end up by defeating yourself and feeling cheated and angry.

It does no good to fight negative thoughts that may spring up; dismiss them and give them no room or energy to distract you.

Our motives for affirming must spring from a desire to change our lives and our consciousness, to become what we want; then the negative thoughts will drop by the wayside. Place your whole attention on the thought you are affirming. Remember it is your decision that determines what thoughts you focus on; to the degree you use this concentration, your

affirmations will be successful. Focus until you succeed in establishing what you are affirming in your consciousness. Then it will materialize in your life. You need to believe you can manifest it. Doubt is like digging up seeds you have planted to see if they have sprouted. Continue affirming, believing that you are changing what you want to change in your life.

Affirmation Guidelines

When using affirmations remember these important rules:

1. The affirmation needs to be intellectually or intelligently understood and emotionally felt.
2. Concentration on a thought produces a magnetic field of energy.
3. The affirmation needs to be repeated with a devotional attitude of desire for truth and spiritual attainment.
4. Visualize what you are affirming. See in your mind's eye that the Light of God is surrounding you—an aura of healing light. Then picture yourself having that which is affirmed.
5. Let go of all distractions and limitations. Rise above them.
6. Be patient and gentle with yourself, using a joyous attitude.
7. Claim your birthright as a child of God. Feel His love and acceptance.

Materialized Affirmations

As we go deeper and deeper in meditation or affirmations we progress from the conscious through the subconscious to the superconscious mind. The vibration of the affirmation can then call a response from the Universal Storehouse. Conscious and subconscious repetition will gradually change into superconscious realization, and you can then materialize what is confidently affirmed. It is a spiritual law and the one that underlies systems of positive thinking.

It is the life force within your body that heals. When the affirmation reaches the superconscious mind, then the intelligent life force within you is spontaneously activated, causing bodily discomforts, negative thought forms, or spiritual ignorance to be removed from the temple of your consciousness.

When and How to Practice Affirmations

Affirmations are best practiced just before going to bed and upon waking in the morning. Assume whatever position is comfortable for you. It is best if the spine is straight and relaxed and the mind is alert. You may wish to concentrate on a point between the eyebrows,* gazing gently with eyes closed. Still the restless conscious mind. Quiet the fanciful subconscious. Invoke the all-powerful superconsciousness by concentrating deeply. Repeat the affirmation out loud, then mentally or softly repeat it again and again until you are saturated with its truth and vibration. Repeat the affirmation throughout the day whenever it comes to mind. Writing it out several times improves its effectiveness. It is most effective if you use your chosen affirmation for 21 days so that it becomes firmly established.

Chart Study: Winning As a Way of Life

In our next chart we have several examples of transforming attitudes through affirmations. Study the chart, take whatever inspiring thoughts you feel will work for you, and make them your own.

*"If therefore Thine eye be single, thy whole body shall be full of Light." Matthew 6:22

WINNING AS A WAY OF LIFE

Sense Pleasures	Transforming Affirmations	Soul Pleasures
Attract by offering easy pleasures, which ultimately destroy happiness. →	Finding the Joy within is more rewarding than giving in to any outward temptation. →	At first harder to obtain but ultimately leading to superior, lasting happiness.
↓		↓
Sense-controlled mind chooses attitudes, circumstances, and actions that lead to:		Inner soul chooses attitudes, circumstances and actions that lead to:
↓		↓
Negative thoughts* →	Affirm and manifest the opposite quality in thought, word, and deed. →	Creative thoughts
Downgrading actions* →	Practice moderation in everything. Listen to the wisdom of your inner self. Compare and choose the satisfaction from life-promoting actions. If subject to temptation, remove yourself from its influence. →	Actions that leave us feeling good about ourselves
Sorrow* →	Feel the joy of winning within and turn to positive interaction with humanity. Meet obstacles with a smile and determination. →	Happiness
Egotism* →	Realize that you cannot exist without the life energy of Spirit. God is supreme yet He works in silence, creating the beautiful. Choose something larger than yourself to align with. →	Gaining a real sense of your worth and ability to contribute
Selfishness* →	Look upon all mankind as part of your greater, expanded self. What we do for others will be returned to us according to cosmic law. In helping others we are given an opportunity to work out our salvation and gain happiness and satisfaction. →	Joyous unselfishness
Hatred* →	Do not wish for others anything that is contrary to your own good. See everyone as a child of God, and decide to be part of all that is bringing in a better life. →	Love
Anger* →	Anger is a disease and is the method of fools. Affirm peace, love, and forgiveness. See all mankind as brothers who often hurt one another. Forgive yourself for striking out and then you can forgive others for doing the same. →	Peace, calm understanding

*There is no need to fear negative thoughts or emotions in your consciousness. Look at them, understand them, and you can then transform them.

SUGGESTED AFFIRMATIONS

I now choose to amplify all my strengths.

If I have something to overcome
I concentrate on the opposite quality of the soul.
I affirm love over hatred,
Peace over restlessness, joy over sorrow.

I focus on my positive qualities, thereby diminishing and leaving behind the undesirable ones.

I am a worthy person, heir(ess) to the abundance of the universe.

Influences on Behaviour

It is important to understand how different daily impressions affect our consciousness. This knowledge will help us to put our affirmations to better use and gain the maximum benefit.

OUTER ENVIRONMENT

Remember that we have choice and free will. We choose when we receive impressions from within or without. Outward stimulation comes from the senses as they contact the world of matter. One can feel pleasure or pain from contact with the material world. Family influences and companions encourage us or erode our self-esteem. The books we read can uplift us or bring us down. It is therefore very important that we surround ourselves with spiritual and moral people and choose uplifting pastimes and reading material. Having a positive outer environment is supremely important if we wish to gain the maximum benefit from our affirmations.

INNER ENVIRONMENT

From the inner realms, consciousness is affected by past-life tendencies and also early-life conditioning, habits, and attitudes ingrained often before we were aware enough to choose. Our character is the result of our thoughts and habit patterns established over a period of many years. We are the sum total of everything we have thought and done. Through choices and our thoughts we are the architects of our personalities and bodies. We have been instrumental in creating our attributes and strengths as well as our deficiencies and weaknesses. Our vibrational pattern is the sum total of what we have done in the past and what we have created up to now. This pattern is the guiding force that draws us to certain people and situations. It determines where and what we are right now.

Since we have created everything we are and have attracted to ourselves all the problems we must face, we can change the pattern. In most cases, however, we will need to make a deter-

mined and ongoing effort to remove unwanted tendencies since these patterns are deeply rooted and seem like second nature. The key is a determined and gentle perseverance with a resolve to try and try again. What we have created thus far has taken a lot of time and effort to build. If we wish to change it, we must be willing to put in the same amount of effort with an attitude of optimism and determination.

The positive soul qualities emanating from the superconscious mind are also an internal influence. If one makes a reasonable effort over a period of time to better oneself, a response will be felt from the superconscious. When that happens one will become aware of the treasure house of joyous divine qualities we all have within, and undesirable tendencies will begin to fall away.

The greater satisfaction will make the temporary pleasures of the senses lose their appeal.

Chart Study: Influences on Behaviour

The following chart of influences on behaviour is a representation of the various factors that affect consciousness. Review this chart and determine what factors are influencing your life. If they are disturbing, then you can adopt measures to change them.

If some outward source is a disruptive influence and it is not immediately possible to remove it, then try to rise above it. If unwanted past thoughts and habit patterns strongly influence your life, then stop feeding these negative patterns and begin to replace them with positive affirmations and actions. The ultimate goal is to create a positive and tranquil inner environment to give us unshakable security so that we can cope with and be master of the circumstances that surround us.

INFLUENCES ON BEHAVIOUR

Negative Influences from Environment & Company

↓

World and Associates

Materialistic social and business trends and habits of people with whom we interact. Those who put emphasis on all the negative things that are going on.

Family Influence

Discouraging comments especially during the formative years of childhood and lack of support and encouragement as well as ridicule or scornful, demeaning remarks.

Books

Sensationalism that stimulates the imagination, passions, and desires. Gloomy and pessimistic reports of crime, violence, and perversion. Hate literature. Nationalism that fosters fear and suspicion, pessimism, distortion, and despair.

Negative Influence from Within / Positive Influence from Within

↓

Subconscious Influences

Conditioning from childhood not assimilated by the conscious mind. This can be painful and negative or encouraging and confidence-building.

↓

Buried memories of painful events. Feelings of guilt or self-scorn. Phobias or destructive habits.

or

Good habits such as the ability to concentrate or to discriminate. Positive feelings of self-worth. Talents or abilities that have been developed, a sunny personality or a loving disposition and a sense of humour.

↓

Innate or inherited tendencies or attitudes, some, perhaps, brought over from other lives.

plus

Positive Soul Qualities

↓

Positive Influences from Environment & Company

↓

World and Associates

Spiritual movements and outstanding leaders and people that encourage us with their examples. Networks that let us know all the positive things being done and constructive steps being taken to end hunger, poverty, and the causes of war.

Family Influence

Encouraging comments and experiences during childhood, allowing us to learn and grow in wisdom and confidence in our own abilities. Support and understanding among friends and family.

Books

Guidelines from uplifting experiences, techniques or inspiration for spiritual growth. Examples from the lives of great leaders. Scriptures and books of wisdom; art, music, and science.

Positive and Negative Forces That Influence the Conscious Mind

SUGGESTED AFFIRMATIONS

**I give thanks for all the inner abilities
I am able to manifest in my life.**

**As I attune myself to the highest within me,
I am protected from any negativity around me.**

**I overcome and heal with ease limiting beliefs,
Old admonitions, and destructive programming.
I am drawing peace and prosperity to me.**

**I take time to consider alternatives and make decisions wisely.
I stay firm in following my inner decision no matter what obstacles present themselves.**

**Each moment calls for decisions;
Demands are made from inner and outer realms.
I choose positive, uplifting vibrations,
Leading me to Self-Realization and inner Joy.**

Choosing What We Want to Become

SENSATIONS PRODUCE THOUGHTS

In order to become a master of life it is necessary to become master of our thoughts. Impressions from senses travel along nerve channels to the brain, where they may be converted into perceptions, conceptions, and then thoughts.

THOUGHT CONTROLS FEELING

If nerves are frozen, as is done in the practice of dentistry, then the sensation of the grinding drill cannot travel to the brain, so there is no thought connection to allow a reaction of displeasure or feeling victimized. Through the practice of introspection we can realize that emotions spring from thought. When we feel bodily discomfort we think we are sick, and the ensuing emotion amplifies the discomfort. If we think someone has mistreated us, then we will feel anger. If we think a situation is sad, then we will cry.

SUBCONSCIOUS CONDITIONING

If we can control our thought process, then we can be in control of our emotions and not be swept away by them. From thought comes emotional feelings, and from these feelings springs action. To think, feel, and act on an experience enough times causes it to become automatic. Once we have created a strong habit of reacting, it becomes a personality or character trait. When a pattern is firmly established, it becomes rooted in the subconscious mind and we are then conditioned, and the reaction seems to come without our volition. Our gift of free will and choice is clouded by the programming of the subconscious. Someone says something, and we react. A sensation plays on our senses, and we respond automatically.

This conditioning is positive if it is under control and prevents us from danger. If we put our hand on a stove knowing it could be hot, then the automatic response of pulling our hand off when it is, is good. An automatic

reaction is not conducive to well-being if it works against our best interests. If, for example, someone says something we think is disparaging and we immediately become angry or hurt and lash out at that person, then this conditioning is not to our advantage.

Master of Life

In order to be in charge of our lives we need to have a calm mind, free from uncontrolled responses. As impressions and the resulting thoughts are received, a masterful person can remain detached and analyze them one at a time. A person who is not in charge of himself is bombarded with impressions and often immediately reacts upon them, not even being aware of what these impressions and thoughts are—just reacting through subconscious conditioning. A master is constantly aware of the flow of impressions and thoughts passing through his mind and responds appropriately or not at all. If it is conducive to his welfare or to the benefit of others, then he will respond. If there are inharmonious impressions, a masterful person will not allow them to be translated into inharmonious feelings and actions.

Chart: We Become What We Choose

Study the next chart with the realization that thought is the main controller of our feelings, actions, and habits. With this realization we can see that by calming our minds and using Creative Thought Remedies or affirmations we can live our lives by choice instead of by reacting to whatever comes.

CHOOSING WHAT WE WANT TO BECOME

Negativity
(Restlessness–bitterness–sorrow)

Craving for sensual pleasures. Attachments to transient gratifications. Negative company, environment, books. Destructive habits that ride rough-shod over nature, animals, and people.

Positivity
(Peace–love–joy)

Realizing and affirming our uniqueness and place in the Divine Plan. Soul guidance through meditation and prayer. Uplifting company, environment, books. Harmonizing with nature and tuning into our oneness with all life.

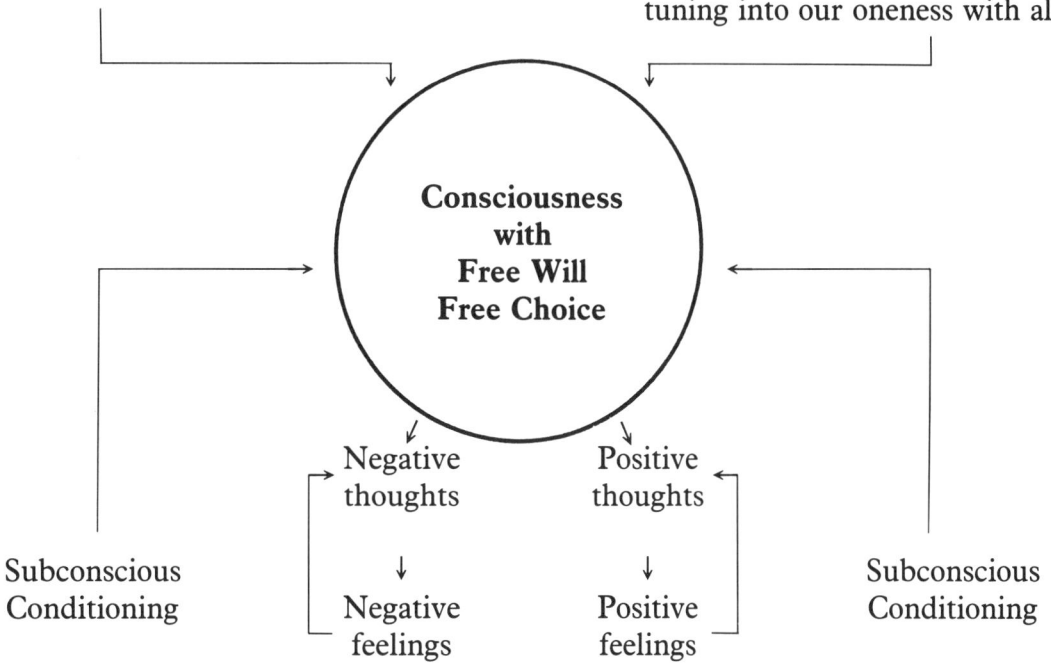

Consciousness with Free Will Free Choice

Subconscious Conditioning

Preoccupation with whims, moods, pride, prejudice, rationalizations about why we are right, feelings of unworthiness, anger, edginess, readiness to strike out or get revenge, self-justification and insensitivity to other's feelings, anticipation of rejection.

Subconscious Conditioning

Innate yearning to better ourselves and grow. Intuitive yearning to realize oneness with Spirit. Desire to be useful and help others. Awe and love of nature's beauty. Sense of upliftment and creative inspiration in times of harmony or in the presence of beauty.

Negative thoughts → Negative feelings → Actions / Repetition of Actions → Negative habits → Character → Restlessness, sorrow, bitterness, hurt, and pain.

Positive thoughts → Positive feelings → Actions / Repetition of Actions → Positive habits → Character → Peace, love, joy, well-being.

SUGGESTED AFFIRMATIONS

    I now realize how important my daily decisions are.
Each choice I now make leads me toward my own best good.

In the calmness of my mind
I watch the ceaseless flow of my thoughts;
I pluck and manifest only those flowers
That bring something constructive to myself and my fellow man.

I am a master of my life;
The thoughts I choose to act on
From the impressions I receive
Are thoughts of harmony and love.

Moment by moment I see my choices
Bring me the results I wish for in my life.

I am taking charge of my life.
I choose each day to make my life worthwhile.

Disturbing Thoughts and Emotions

ROOT CAUSES

When we analyze ourselves it is necessary to come face to face with our destructive patterns. Suppression of disruptive thoughts and feelings is not a method that will transform them. Suppression only causes emotions to build up inside until enough pressure is generated that we explode at some trivial provocation. This process can alienate us from friends and family and even lead to a breakdown.

Ignoring negative thoughts and emotions while concentrating on positive thoughts and affirmations may not be successful in all cases. Very often we may have to weed out the destructive tendencies before it is effective to use Creative Thought Affirmations. Through introspection we can trace problems back to the root cause and remove them through understanding them and forgiving ourselves and anyone involved. For example, a person may analyze himself and find that the seed cause of his insecurities came from many unsupportive comments made by his parents. Realizing this, he can then see that he is really a person of worth and can understand that his parents thought they were doing their duty and did not realize the effect they had on him. If he can forgive them—and himself for resenting this—he is then free to see himself as a good person and affirm his own goodness and worth.

UNSUBSTANTIAL EMOTIONS

It is also important to understand that most fears have no substantial basis. We have unwittingly given them authority when they had no real foundation. By the process of introspection some people may find that they fear the feelings of fear, anger, or depression. Through going into these feelings rather than avoiding them they can often discover that energy tied up in the fear is the attractive force that draws the disturbing emotion into their consciousness. The fear thought may even control them to the extent that they freeze or become paralyzed and cannot think or act properly. Some people even get to a

point where they are afraid to think, for they believe that everything within themselves is destructive.

If we closely examine our thoughts and feelings with a sense of detachment, we can trace them back to childhood and realize that there is really no substantial basis for our reactions and can thus free ourselves from those feelings. Then we can freely affirm our real beingness.

During a period in my own life I was experiencing some deep fears and decided to analyze them. For weeks I watched them closely and began to write down their patterns (see Making a Personal Thought Remedy Chart at the end of the book). I was determined to get to the root cause of these emotions that had been crippling me. I followed the pattern as far as I could, hoping to find an all-important revelation. I searched for a long time but could not put my finger on the root cause. One day I had an intuitive realization that there was no root cause at all and that I had built a pyramid of thoughts and emotions out of nothing substantial. In this complex jungle of thoughts and emotions I had created an unrealistic fear. With this understanding the fear dissipated. It is important to understand that fear is nothing real. It is taking something unpleasant from the past, expecting that it might happen in the future, and then experiencing all the feelings that it could bring, and so avoiding or trying to prevent some situation that *might* arise.

If we reflect on this, isn't it silly to upset our bodies and spoil the now with unpleasant feelings about something that only *might* happen in the future? What important and positive experiences we may be turning away from just because something might happen! Remember that what we focus on, we draw to us. Why draw to us unpleasant things we do not want? Affirm safety and positive experiences to draw them to you, and you can dare to live your life as you want to.

CHART STUDY: DISTURBING THOUGHTS AND EMOTIONS

In the last section of our book (Making a Personal Thought Remedy Chart) you, the reader, are shown how to meet your disruptive feelings head on and eliminate them. In the Thought Remedy Chart that follows is delineated the way disturbing thoughts and emotions can affect and limit us. With this knowledge we can untie the binding strings that these emotions place on our consciousness, allowing us to experience the innate freedom that is our birthright.

DISTURBING THOUGHTS AND EMOTIONS

↓

Entertaining negative feelings such as fear, jealousy, anger, resentment, hurt feelings, etc.

↓

Ties up energy and consciousness in negative reactions and emotions.

↓

Paralyzes me so it is difficult to discriminate.

↓

Inhibits creative ability and true intuitive understanding.

↓

Overpowers and suppresses worthwhile and uplifting feelings.

↓

Boggles the will and results in inefficient effort in all endeavours.

↓

Radiates to others, making it seem impossible to get along with them.

↓

Increases frustration and anger, which make the cycle more powerful and self-perpetuating.

↓

SUGGESTED AFFIRMATIONS

I am master of my life and my feelings;
I am making each day what I want it to be.

I know that my state of being affects those around me;
I choose to be a center of calm that radiates to all I meet.

As I experience the trembling of fear, the tears of sadness, or the powers of anger,
    I let them go, heal, and return to my true nature of peace.

Behind all conditioning,
Behind all objects,
Behind all thoughts is peace.
I am rising above all conditioning, objects, and thoughts;
I am enveloped in peace.

Let nothing but good flow from me;
Let nothing but good come to me.

Part Two

WHAT PROMOTES AND WHAT DIMINISHES JOYOUS LIVING

Damaging Habits Are the Mud Covering the Gold of the Soul.
Goodness Is the Radiance of the Soul.

Self-Deprecation or Self-Confidence

IMAGE OF GOD

We are all children of God; each of us is special in the eyes of the Father. Not only has He created us; He has made us in His own Image. Our consciousness is Spirit itself, for everything is a manifestation of the One. *Made in the Image of God* means we are divine, holy beings and have the potential to manifest our Godlike natures.

Everyone has been given individuality, and within each being is a treasure house of inner divine qualities. We have enough power and wisdom to solve and accomplish any task that comes our way. We have the unconditional love of God within us and can value and love ourselves and every part of His creation. If we were to release all our innate joy, we could radiate smiles throughout the universe.

We are unique. Spirit has taken a special moment in time to create each one of us. Our consciousness is indestructible and will exist for eternity. We always were and will always be a living soul. We are each necessary to the universe, for without us the universe is incomplete. Our consciousness is a part of what makes the universe whole.

In our created uniqueness and individuality Spirit has given each of us special gifts or affinity to some of God's divine qualities. The purpose of our existence is to manifest our special uniqueness in order to fulfill our role and join our Creator in the uplifting of humanity.

God is proud of every aspect of His creation. He wants each of us to feel our connection to the whole and work together in harmony. Since the Creator is proud of each creation, then we as His created offspring need to be proud of ourselves. Any thought, feeling, or action that downgrades our innate worth is error and brings misery. Any identification with self-deprecation, guilt, despair over mistakes, or insecurities is false reasoning. We are God's children, and all we have to do is remove our self-imposed limitations and those placed upon us by our conditioning.

We have infinite potential, and if we had a glimpse of this, we would spontaneously bow our heads in gratitude at the feet of the Divine. With so much given to us, it is of paramount importance that we make it an experienced reality.

CHART STUDY: SELF-DEPRECATION OR SELF-CONFIDENCE

As you study the following chart, realize your own uniqueness and divine nature. Let go the cloud of limiting thoughts and experiences and stand tall in the sun of your own worth.

SELF-DEPRECATION OR SELF-CONFIDENCE

Self-Defeating Behaviour

False humility that does not acknowledge my own worth as a child of God.

Feeling unworthy of God or anything good in creation.

Suppressing inner qualities of the soul.

Feeling I should not express my inner creativity and joy.

Feeling that I cannot achieve a certain goal or that a task is beyond my capacity to handle, thereby shirking it and giving up a chance for growth.

Putting others' opinions ahead of my own.

Seeking the approval of others instead of my own inner direction. Not listening to my inner guidance.

Overidentification with mistakes and guilt, thus losing sight of my God nature. Not really taking responsibility for myself and putting my life in order and my abilities to work.

Not enjoying the universe that God created for us to experience and to use for our needs and growth.

Concentrating on sorrow and suffering, which are not qualities of the soul.

Indulging in practices that limit me so that I experience only negativity instead of the beauty and grandeur and warmth and sharing that are there in God's world for *me* to enjoy and bring into fuller expression.

Self-Acceptance—Self-Confidence

Spirit took a special time to create me. I am unique—a masterpiece of His creation, and He is proud of me and wants me to be proud of my own worth and abilities and to put them to work for a better world.

The universe is incomplete without me and my special uniqueness.

I have a gift that no one else has, and my purpose on earth is to manifest my own special beingness and use it for the benefit of all.

I am a child of God made in His Divine Image.

Creativity, wisdom, power, love and joy are within me, ready to be awakened and manifested.

I do not need to acquire anything from without—all potential is within me, waiting to be discovered.

God is the universe of love; being made in His Image, I too am the universe of love.

I am a creator as my Father is, and there is no task that comes my way that is beyond my capacity to perform. Power is already within me for whatever each day brings.

SUGGESTED AFFIRMATIONS

> I stand tall in the sun of my own uniqueness;
> I am unconditionally loved by my Creator.
> I stand tall in the moon of my own worth;
> I can give unconditional love to all who cross my path.
>
> I am attuning to my own creativity and talents;
> I freely express the beauty of my inner self.
>
> Not a sparrow falls to the ground
> Without the Heavenly Father knowing.
> I am seen, I am known, I am loved
> By Him who created me.
>
> I have qualities and talents that the world needs;
> I choose to develop and give these to humanity.

Desires

Wheel of Life

Life is like a perpetually rotating wheel. A soul that is unaware that it is on this wheel must incarnate again and again. The reincarnation cycle will never cease until the soul discovers the cord that binds it to the revolving wheel of sensory life.

Desire is the force that keeps our energy bound to the world of sensations. Desire is the root cause of our attachment to material things and the cycle of reincarnation. If consciousness sees something that it believes will give it happiness, it continually thinks of it and pursues it until the desired object is obtained. As long as there are unfulfilled desires and strong attachments to things of this world in our consciousness, then the soul must be reborn again and again until that desire is fulfilled.

Fulfill Desires through Experience

If we wish to remove ourselves from this ceaseless pattern, there is a way of escape, and that is to remove desire. There are, however, several ways of releasing the soul from the chain of desire. The longer and more encumbering method is to satisfy all our desire by experiencing them. When we have experienced them all and the heart is satisfied then one is no longer compelled to reincarnate. There is a problem here, however, for not only are there physical desires but astral and causal as well. Spirit has created three spheres of existence: the grosser physical realm, the astral realm of light, and the causal realm of thought. "In my Father's house are many mansions" (John 14:2). After a soul has spent numerous incarnations satisfying its physical desires, then it has to satisfy the more refined astral and causal ones. This may sound fine in theory, but when we stop to understand how much anxiety, frustration, disappointment, and suffering must be experienced before we can satisfy all these desires, we will intuitively look for a better way.

Releasing Desire through Wisdom and Understanding

The best method is to observe all these desires with the magnifying glass of wisdom. By observation we can see that many of the

things people are running after do not bring either satisfaction or happiness. We may realize from our own experience that satisfying one desire only awakens another and that the process is endless. Wisdom will show us that it is virtually impossible for the gratification found in a changing, fleeting world to satisfy our inner changeless soul.

Transforming Desire through God Contact

The most effective method to change our lives is to enter within and begin to feel the satisfying presence of our connection to all of creation and the Creator. Christ tells us to seek first the kingdom of God and all things will be added unto us. In the exalted state of God Consciousness the heart is completely satisfied and there is no need to seek anything outside oneself. Seeking God first, we will ultimately find that all our lesser wholesome desires have been fulfilled. In this state we can enjoy God's creation without being all entangled in it. Seeing the presence of God in all things, we can do our work in the world and not be enslaved. This is real freedom.

Chart Study: Desire

In reviewing our next chart you can see the benefits and limitations of certain forms of desire. Analyze your own patterns and determine which desires are serving you and aiding your progress and which ones are preventing you from achieving your highest potential.

DESIRES

Take inventory of your desires to determine which uplift and which downgrade you.

Material Desires

Material desires can never satisfy the soul's longing for union with God. Most people blindly fulfill one desire after another in search of ultimate happiness that is never found.

Any desire that prevents me from cultivating my inner soul qualities and returning to Spirit is negative and quenches my potential.

Whatever I desire or do that is not in accordance with the inner dictates of my soul and God is bound to defeat me and leave me unfulfilled.

Attachment to my body creates material desires that direct energy outward to the senses to fulfill desires that are never satisfied.

Many influences nourish material desires within us. If we see something we like, the desire revolves in our minds and plagues us with its joy-expecting thought, which we follow like the pot of gold at the end of the rainbow.

If the desire for money causes me to lie and cheat, or attachment to food causes me to eat in greed, then my soul qualities are smothered with these negative qualities.

If I die with the desire for material things in my heart, then I will have to reincarnate on earth again to fulfill them.

Spiritual Desires

The Desire to Know God Brings the Greatest Fulfillment.

Seek ye first the kingdom of God and His righteousness and all these things shall be added unto you. (Matthew 6:33)

All things that I desire, the love I seek in others, the wisdom I seek in books will all be found in God.

This impermanent, changing world can never satisfy the changeless soul. It is only through contact with the changeless Spirit that my soul can experience complete satisfaction and fulfillment.

My inner quest to know my true connection to all that is changeless will bring me peace, love, and joy.

I enjoy the good things in life and elevate my desires with thoughts of God and the awareness of His presence in all things.

I will find freedom from compulsion and inner turmoil as I take my place doing my part in the upliftment of humanity.

SUGGESTED AFFIRMATIONS

>Following desires of the moment leaves me empty and unsatisfied;
>I choose now the path of moderation and fulfillment.
>
>More and more I am attuning my desires to the Will of God.
>
>I renounce all limiting desires
>And rest in God's Unconditional Love.
>
>More and more the Divine Way is my way.
>My desires are purified by Spirit.

Creative Attitudes

BEGIN WITH SMALL ACCOMPLISHMENTS

In order to overcome fear it is necessary to concentrate on its opposites—confidence and courage. It is helpful to hold thought affirmations of these qualities uppermost in our minds. In the beginning we need to take small steps and celebrate small accomplishments since confidence grows through achievements. It is best to set out a small realistic program and practice it until definite results are achieved. It is futile to try to accomplish a goal that is beyond your capacity at your particular stage of development.

In the initial stages of enthusiasm the tendency often is to pick a high and lofty goal that will be nearly impossible to manifest. If success is not forthcoming, then we may become discouraged and give up altogether. This in turn will tend to add fuel to existing fear and self-doubt and make it harder to begin again to accomplish objectives. Be true and fair to yourself and choose something that you know you can accomplish through the use of courage, affirmation, and sincere effort. As you achieve small successes you are able to challenge and accomplish larger tasks. In time you will find that no worthy goal is beyond your capacities.

LATENT POTENTIAL WITHIN

As children of God, heirs to the power of Spirit, we have the capacity to accomplish whatever we put our heart, soul, and mind into. Everything that Christ and the Masters manifested we too can manifest. If we develop ourselves and make ourselves receptive, then the universe and all the laws of nature will work with us.

Science tells us that mankind is using only a small fraction of its brain capacity. Within us is all the potential we need. It is a matter of realizing this and allowing it to unfold. Even sublime qualities are already latent within us. There is only one way: we have to convince ourselves through experience. We can accom-

plish this by choosing goals and working toward them and developing ourselves in a gradual, step-by-step unfoldment. We can begin where we are and go on to accomplish better and more lofty things until we at last may realize we have become Christlike, Krishnalike, Buddhalike. Then we will understand that by steadily unfolding our capacities we have come to realize our own divinity and can help others realize theirs.

Attributes and Their Double-Edged Characteristics

There is an old saying that any virtue overdone becomes a vice. When working with positive and destructive qualities it is of paramount importance to remember that a positive quality overdone can turn into a destructive one, and a destructive one can have positive implications. A good example of this is the experience that Saint Teresa of Avila shares with us in her autobiography. She relates that even though she was going into ecstasy and Jesus Christ was appearing to her, still she gave up prayer and meditation for a year and a half, because of the thought of her unworthiness to behold the presence of Jesus. Saint Teresa conveys to us that she felt that her practice of humility was noble, but through the help of a counsellor she came to understand that this was false humility that was denying her own spiritual nature.

There are numerous other examples of misusing a virtue and creating a vice. Under the guise of humility some people deny their own abilities and worth and indulge in all sorts of insecurities and fears. Others practice the virtue of service to others with such force and enthusiasm that they intrude on the privacy and will of others and are not serving but being a nuisance. One may practice renunciation to such a degree that he ruins his health and as a result can no longer meditate properly or serve others. Others may so discipline themselves that they completely obliterate the childlike, joyous spirit of their souls. Some practice confidence and courage so zealously that all they manifest is their own egos to lord it over others.

Honest Introspection

The keynote in enhancing your life is to keep your focus on an all-round, balanced development through honest introspection. Spiritually, it is important that one be true to oneself and to God. The key factors are motives and attitudes. If you are pure in heart and offer your thoughts and actions up to God, praying for guidance, then you will find your way to joy and fulfillment.

Chart Study: Creative Attitudes

Our next chart reviews many of the fears that people experience and positive recipes for courage and soul progress. As stated, the experience of fear blocks positive manifestations. Let us look at how we can use the experience of fear for our ultimate benefit. Then we can review other aspects of fear that we need to become aware of and transform. If in the following chart you relate to one or more of the fear experiences, then the Positive Thought Remedy can aid you in releasing yourself from, and transforming, that fear.

CREATIVE ATTITUDES

Fears That Can Serve to Caution You	Recipes for Courage and Soul Progress
Loving fear	→ We need to be on guard to avoid breaking the laws of God, not from fear of punishment, but because we love Him and wish to co-create with Him a better world.
Constructive fear	→ It is good to be calmly watchful of our actions so that we do not hurt someone unnecessarily.
Cautious fear	→ This fear is a protection that helps us avoid situations that are dangerous to our well-being. It prevents us from a reckless lifestyle and overindulgence in the senses, which lead to ill health and unhappiness.
Fear of destructive actions	→ God is on your side, and if you make a sincere effort and trust in Him, you will not fail. You will be able to overcome destructive habits and move away from associates that draw you back into limiting old patterns. It is good to visualize the lives of saints who have overcome and follow their uplifting example.
Fear of prideful thoughts	→ Humility is the virtue most pleasing to Spirit, and if egotistical thoughts well up in our minds, they cause pain to the soul. Do not react to them; just understand their absurdity. God has created you as a unique entity and loves you unconditionally. True humility is in knowing your own special worth but realizing that without God's blessing you cannot think or act. See God as the sole doer in the universe and consider it a privilege to use the gifts He has bestowed on you. Cosmic Consciousness is the awareness of every particle of the created universe and the vibrationless void beyond. How can we possibly entertain any conceit when we realize how far we are from a perfected state of consciousness?
Fear of negative vibrations (emotions of others)	→ Mentally surround yourself with the Light of Spirit and affirm, "I am protected in the Light of God." Merge in Spirit and make your vibration stronger than any around you.
Fear of not pleasing others	→ Remember no one can please all the people all the time. Even the greatest masters were misunderstood and had their enemies. Do your best to be kind and loving to all mankind, and dismiss your anxiety and leave it in God's hands.

Negative Fears	**Recipes for Courage and Soul Progress**

General fears → When you contact your true inner essence fears will leave your heart, for fear cannot exist in the purifying vibration of Spirit.

    SUGGESTED AFFIRMATION:
    I am Divinely guided and protected.

Fear of failure → As a Child of God made in His Image, you have infinite power behind you to overcome all stumbling stones. Look at all problems as opportunities for you to conquer and grow materially, mentally, and spiritually. Focus not on the emotions and feelings, but on ways of solving or overcoming. Meditate constructively on any troubling situation and you will find a way to use it in your growth.

    SUGGESTED AFFIRMATION:
    I achieve with ease all that is important to me.

Fear of Making Mistakes → This is something we take on in childhood as if it were a sin. Mistakes show us what to avoid now. We can absorb their lessons and then forget them. Nothing is gained by dwelling on them.

    SUGGESTED AFFIRMATION:
    Mistakes serve to show me where my actions have not served me.
    I learn from them and let associated guilt feelings go.

Fear of rejection → God loves us unconditionally no matter what we do, for we are His children. God never pushes us away but is continuously trying to bring us back to Him. It is we who push God away by our indifference and focus on worldly things. Open your heart to the infinite love of God and you will know that He is love and that He loves you always. Convey that divine love to all whom you meet, and they will be drawn to you and in time consider it a privilege to be with you. Everyone responds to love that comes from the heart. No one will reject that.

    SUGGESTED AFFIRMATION:
    As a child of God, I am worthy of the highest good.

Fear of oneself (negative thoughts and feelings) → Confront your timidities and uncertainties fearlessly and they will dissapear. We do not really create thoughts—they are already there in the ether. Our consciousness attracts certain thoughts, and we have free will to choose and experience whatever thoughts and emotions we wish. Do not fear thoughts but choose the highest and the best. Rather than suppress, replace thoughts or emotions with ones you enjoy and want. With practice the unwanted ones will no longer come.

    SUGGESTED AFFIRMATION:
    I accept myself as I am and grow daily in my Divine purpose.

Fear of one's conscience and guilt feelings → Your conscience is one of the greatest protections and friends you have, for it is the voice of God. It tells you what does not serve your best interests. The deeper you grow in consciousness the sharper your conscience will be, and it will let you know when you are off the mark. Do not fear your conscience or guilt feelings. Listen to them and evaluate what it is they are telling you. Once you have learned what they have to teach, do not wallow in guilt. Change what needs changing and then get on with new, fulfilling ways of living. God forgives us instantly. We must forgive ourselves.

    SUGGESTED AFFIRMATION:
    When I feel guilty, I pause to understand, forgive, and let go,
    and I find the blessing from the learning.

Negative Fears	Recipes for Courage and Soul Progress

Fear of disease and pain → Fear attracts the very thing being feared. If you dwell on a particular ailment, you will become more susceptible to it no matter what method you use to prevent it. When your heart is filled with fear your will is paralyzed, and so the body's vitality and immune system are lowered, and disease germs are more able to invade. Study and follow health laws, then forget dangers to the body. Center on things that uplift you. Concentrate on the changeless, diseaseless, and painless soul.

SUGGESTED AFFIRMATION:
In my being there is no disease, pain, or death;
I am healed, balanced, harmonized, and attuned.

Fear of death → Death comes to everyone, regardless of status, position or creed. The soul never dies; it only changes its bodily costume and roles at death. See death as a birth into a new life with new opportunities to grow. Be fully in the moment and leave your death in God's hands. Have faith in Him. Know that as you do His work, your future in eternity is secure.

SUGGESTED AFFIRMATION:
At death the physical cloak is shed and the soul soars free.

Fear of the unknown → Meditate and realize that the invisible realms are as real as the visible and that the universe is a safe and friendly place. Fear only strangles you and makes you impotent. Trust tomorrow to be better than today as you grow into light. As you do this, it will become so, and you will realize that what you feared had no substance.

SUGGESTED AFFIRMATION:
I trust more completely in the love of God to guide me on my way.

Fear of change → All of creation is in a state of motion or change, and nothing remains stationary. If we analyze each moment in time we will find that we are either progressing or regressing. Do not let fear take you backward. Change yourself and grow in consciousness toward a better way.

SUGGESTED AFFIRMATION:
Nothing stays the same. Change is a condition of life.
I gladly meet the challenges of today, tomorrow, and the future.

Fear of your actions in associating with others → God has taken the time and care to create you as a unique soul, different from any other. Be proud of your individuality. If your divine treasures are stored away and unused, brush off the dust of bad habits and let them come forth. People need the qualities you have, for the universe is incomplete without you. If you let your inner divine nature flow through you, then the ability to serve and make people happy is at your command.

SUGGESTED AFFIRMATION:
I am looking deeply into myself and my motivation; there is nothing to fear.

SUGGESTED AFFIRMATIONS

When I look closely and deeply at my fears
They fade away, for they have no real substance.

There is nothing to fear; no, nothing to fear.
Fears are delusions, unreal as shadows.
When my will is in accord with the things that last,
I fear nothing, for nothing can harm me.

I proceed with a steady pace over the quicksands of delusion.
I am confident because I know I am a child of God.

Master or Victim

Master Consciousness

Are we masters or victims? Do we control situations and circumstances, or do they control us? A master is in charge of feelings and actions, and all situations are under his control. What someone else says or does will not push him into a display of emotion. A master is one who is guided by wisdom and knows that the goal of life is to realize and express the divine attributes of Spirit.

A master sees and welcomes every situation as the messenger of God or as individualized karma sent to them to help him grow mentally, emotionally and spiritually. A master will seek inner guidance before performing any task. If a master knows that his will is in tune with the Will of God, then he will work calmly and singlemindedly to bring a task to fruition. A master therefore works only to please God and leaves the results of all his actions in God's hands. A master uses the knowledge of life's lessons as stepping stones to perfect his own nature and by example he influences others.

Victim Consciousness

A victim is one who doesn't think about the purpose of life but seeks gratification even at the expense of others. A victim is one who operates from a state of reaction and is unaware of the emotional patterns within his or her self, drifting from one emotion to the next. Victims react impulsively, striking out at others and feeling that they have the right to do so when they feel threatened. Ultimately they will see most situations as threats to their security and will resort to manipulative behaviour patterns to bring about their egocentric goals. Victims feel that life and people are out to get them and will be plunged into helplessness, despair, and frustration when they do not get the results they want.

Chart Study: Master or Victim

In our summary chart we list various attitudes of a master of his life and the characteristics of one who is a victim. Take time to review this chart and find the Creative Thought Remedies or affirmations that will enable you to find your rightful heritage of Master Consciousness.

MASTER OR VICTIM

Victim Consciousness

↓

Reacting instead of sizing up a situation and acting in an appropriate manner.

↓

Feeling that I have a right to explode with anger or fear just because someone says or does something I don't like, thereby allowing others to push a button and be in control of how I feel and act.

↓

Responding with emotions that upset the chemical balance of my body and poison my system.

↓

Seeing all emotion-producing situations as a threat to my being instead of seeing them as opportunities for taking charge.

↓

Holding the belief that emotions just happen and there is nothing I can do about it.

↓

Being unaware that all emotions are goal-oriented behaviour to produce a specific result, and that negative ones usually produce just the opposite of the desired result, and so are self-defeating.

↓

Not recognizing that I create emotions by my belief about a situation, and that the situation is not the cause of my emotion; that it is my belief about it and about how I feel I ought to react, that causes the emotions and the unhappy aftermath.

↓

Feeling that I am a helpless pawn and have no power over myself or my circumstances.

↓

Focussing on what is wrong with my life instead of appreciating what is right and good in it.

Master Consciousness

↓

Knowing that Supreme Intelligence is willing to direct my life so that I may grow to manifest my best nature.

↓

Seeing life as a school and that I am learning lessons in each moment in time and am accepting and profiting by the lesson.

↓

Looking at each emotion-producing situation as an opportunity to grow—a gift, not a threat.

↓

Deciding that each situation is created just for me because I need it for my evolution, and acting on this.

↓

Asking myself in each circumstance, "Is the response I am about to give to this stimulus going to serve me?"

↓

Finding out whether the emotion is something I really want to feel.

↓

If the response serves me and others, I will express it. If it does not, then from a state of maturity and security I will choose one that will.

↓

Owning my own part in drawing each experience to me and finding ways to use it for growth or change.

↓

Deciding to be cheerful or even joyful no matter what the situation and so keeping my life a good experience.

↓

Realizing that I do not help another who is suffering by getting down and wallowing in those feelings but by being there for him and lifting his spirit.

SUGGESTED AFFIRMATIONS

> I am no longer a victim; I am a Cause and a Creator.
>
> I am the Captain of my life; I am the Master of my soul.
>
> I am never blown about by the winds of change
> Or uprooted by storms of worry.
> I live in a calm evenmindedness
> And fulfill God's Will for me.
>
> Mastery is my rightful heritage.
> I choose to take responsibility for all my actions.
> I can handle anything that happens to me.
>
> I am Master of my own soul;
> I sing my own song.
> I am not swayed by the opinions of the masses;
> I follow the inner voice of my own being.

Healing Wisdom

Friends Discuss; Fools Argue

Anger is a destructive emotion, harmful to the nervous system and detrimental to one's health. In a fit of rage chemicals are secreted into the bloodstream that are harmful to us. Even the chemistry of the body, by making us feel bad after, shows us that this is not an emotion that serves us.

Anger never solves a situation; it generally makes it worse. When we angrily challenge someone, we ask for a defensive, angry response. We tend to feel right but not good. The famous saying "friends discuss and fools argue" is sufficient here. When one is in a rage, reason departs and facts are distorted. We are liable to make an enemy and ruin a relationship. It is better to stay detached and graciously remove yourself from the situation until peace and calm return and reason and wisdom can hold sway. If we can see anything that once caused anger as something that neither discredits us nor demeans us, then we can get an objective view of the situation and weigh the consequences of answering in the heat of emotion.

Karma: Universal Justice

Know for certain that if an injustice has been dealt, universal law will dispense its own justice. Everyone reaps what he sows, and whatever has been put out is what will come back. The justice of the universe, or karma, is mathematically sound and exact. There is no action that has not received its due return even if we do not see it. It is not up to us to punish or enlighten another. We need only to look at our own part in the interaction and be sure we have not given another person real cause for hurt.

Through the understanding of karma we also realize that we attract every situation that comes to us through our thoughts and actions. If misfortune comes, it is because we ourselves have created the reason for it. If we have been dishonest, then sometime, somewhere we will

reap the effects. Knowing these principles can help alleviate feelings of anger toward someone who appears to have mistreated us or toward any unfavourable situation that manifests in our lives.

The counsel here is not one of passiveness. The idea is to short-circuit an impulsive and perhaps violent outburst. If an injustice has taken place, then proceed with wisdom and adopt whatever measures are necessary to remedy the situation, but do not compound it with force or anger. If no solution is possible, then surrender it to the wisdom of the universe, and it will be taken care of in its own time.

Chart Study: Healing Wisdom

Our next chart is a study of the various reasons why we experience anger with liberating attitudes and beliefs that can abort it. Anger does have its positive applications and we can sometimes use this emotion for our good.

HEALING WISDOM

Positive Anger	Liberating Thoughts
Spiritual anger	Spiritual precepts are often lost or distorted by intellectual interpretations that have nothing to do with inner realization. Through this practice the teachings of the great Masters have become watered down with dogma, prejudice, and rituals, and the central focus of knowing and loving God has been all but lost. An anger or distaste for spiritual hypocrisy can lead to your betterment if it causes you to seek more deeply until you find and practice successful methods of knowing God and harmonizing your life with changeless values.
Righteous anger (injustice to one's self or to others)	Overcome injustices by noncooperation with the negative ways of others. It is not useful to retaliate. Resist with the superior spiritual force of love. Make the wrongdoing of others a stimulus to live a better life yourself, doing good in this world. There is only one way to counteract negative cruelty and that is by purifying ourselves so we may become channels of light. If your righteous concern leads you to join a spiritual or moral cause, then this is beneficial to you and to the world as long as the group is guided by love and wisdom and not by force.
Transforming anger	Anger can be beneficial if it encourages us to change our bad habits. Being discontent with ourselves can lead us to adopt the best positive measures to change our lives and grow materially, mentally, and spiritually.

Negative Anger

Anger often comes from unfulfilled desires, spiritual or mundane.	Work for the most uplifting cause you can find and leave the results of your actions in God's hands. If obstacles come, calmly persevere and offer them to Spirit. If you are working for God and not yourself, then no opposition can frustrate you or make you angry. If your desires are for the highest good of mankind and your own evolution, then the divine cosmic forces will bring about the circumstances for their manifestation. Conquer anger by removing the source of the problem—desire. Simplify your life and eliminate unnecessary wants so desires no longer disturb your peace of mind.
Anger may come from unfulfilled expectations, spiritual or mundane.	Do not depend on or expect things from others. If their wishes are in opposition to yours, you will feel frustration and anger. Take responsibility for what you do, and use your own creative ability, allowing others theirs. If you allow others to be as they are and put no expectations on their actions, then they can never disappoint you.
Anger may come from receiving criticism from others.	Listen to criticism with an open heart and analyze it to see if the accusations are true. If they are, then change yourself. If the accusations are untrue, show compassion and understanding. Many people try to be tall by belittling others. Do not retaliate; be silent, not as a means of showing displeasure, but to manifest peace. Loving acceptance of another person as he or she is tends to dissolve critical inclinations.

Negative Anger	Liberating Thoughts
Anger may come from the unfaithfulness, arrogance, pushiness, or similar behaviour of others.	Manifest calm understanding and offer kindness from a genuine feeling of sincerity. Do not allow negative behaviour to make you react with negativity too. If necessary, leave the scene as quickly and graciously as possible so that you may have a chance to regain your centre of calm. Give the situation to God and pray, perhaps, "Father forgive them for they know not what they do" (Luke 23:34). The prayer of loving indifference is: "God, he is Thine as I am Thine; help Thou the difference between us."
Anger may come from being blamed for something you did not do.	Shut your eyes to insult, even if it is without reason. It does not pay to strike back with anger or retaliation, for that only escalates the situation. Universal Law will bring about its own justice, and the truth will come to light. If others blame you for something they did themselves, they know in their hearts that they are wrong. Be silent and give them unconditional love, and their consciences will instruct them.
Anger may come from misunderstanding.	If there is a misunderstanding, confront the individual on the matter in a calm, patient, and intelligent manner. Intelligent people discuss their problems, whereas fools argue to win their points. Anger only results in a hot exchange of words, which leads to further misunderstanding and confusion. Truth cannot be found in emotional confrontation.
Anger may come from little annoyances.	Sometimes little things disturb us more than big disasters. This world of duality is far from perfect, and these little annoyances are omnipresent. Mentally we need to rise above distracting influences, giving them no power to upset us.
Anger may come from being ignored.	Change yourself and manifest the positive qualities of love, honesty, humility, and respect. You do not impress anyone by a continuous display of words or acts but simply by being yourself—a beautiful, radiant, soulful being. As others feel the magnetism of your inner qualities, they will naturally be drawn to your vibration.
Anger comes from the feeling that we are losing an argument.	Win others by love and listening to what they have to say. We do not have to be right all the time. There are many people who know much more than we do. Anger never pays, for it only leads to more anger and to the exact opposite of what you are seeking. Argument does not convince another, especially if it contains emotion.
Anger may come from people not changing as we wish.	Use your good example to influence others, not self-righteous words. Nothing annoys people more than a holier-than-thou attitude. Others have the right to be where they are. Realize they are doing what they believe is right for them. We have no right to put our standards and judgments on them. We have enough to do to work on our own shortcomings.

Suggested Affirmations

No matter how people try to provoke me,
I will not provoke back.
No matter how people may treat me,
I will return only love and understanding,
For I am a child of peace.

I use the energy of anger to transform myself.

Anger draws my attention to an opportunity to learn and grow.

Anger can be a defense against sadness and pain.
I now release the pain and heal myself.

Whenever I react with emotion
I analyze it to understand why.
I am learning to recognize and abort strong feelings
Before they carry me away.

Joyousness or Moodiness

INNER PERCEPTIONS

There are many reasons for dark moods, but when the sun of inner perceptions manifests, moods evaporate from one's consciousness.

When we feel inner confidence and work successfully to overcome problems, then the gloom of worry and feelings of helplessness and failure cannot gather. We feel secure when we know that we are making the best possible effort, even when results are not immediately apparent.

When we realize that creation and the material world are not our eternal home, then the winds of misfortune cannot blow us away. The one who enjoys and appreciates God's drama but does not take it too seriously is the happy one.

When we work for the good of all, then the rains of selfishness and indifference will not drown us. We will never feel lazy or bored when we assume the supreme task of helping the Cosmic Creator. If we are calm and lead a simplified life, then the flood of desires does not bother us.

When we meditate and firmly become anchored in the joyous presence of Spirit within, we can permanently rise above all moods.

CHART STUDY: JOYOUSNESS OR MOODINESS

If you find that moods sometimes descend on you, then these Creative Thought Remedies can aid you. Change your thoughts, and the moods will be unable to return.

JOYOUSNESS OR MOODINESS

Ego Consciousness

↓

Moods arise from attitudes and emotions stemming from beliefs of the ego—our little self.

↓

Negative moods are almost always bred from preoccupation with self. Those who think only of themselves are often moody.

↓

Moods come in through the open door of an indifferent state of mind. When we let ourselves feel bored, then we invite moods to play havoc with our peace of mind.

↓

Moods run rampant in minds that are lazy about work or that feel they are too good for work. Both of these attitudes prevent us from fulfilling our potential and finding our rewards. Moods will prevail until we decide to stop avoiding responsibility and get on with living and experiencing.

↓

Negative moods are like dark clouds that encompass us when we feel things are not progressing as we would like. Endless difficulties with one's work and family life, discouragement over ill health, or the feeling of failure all stimulate the negative emotion of moods to mushroom in our consciousness.

↓

Moods are activated if we worry about problems instead of tackling them and working out solutions. We can adopt a triumphant attitude that does not let upsetting emotions in.

Soul Consciousness

↓

Joyousness is an emotion that floods and uplifts our being when we are in touch with and expressing our inner soul qualities. What we entertain in our minds is what we experience. We can decide to experience joy, lightness, success, and they will manifest.

↓

Joyousness is born of the appreciation we feel from noticing our blessings as we are constructively busy and progressing.

↓

Joyousness sings in the heart of him who sees the beauty and marvel of even the tiniest part of God's creation. He that sees and feels the one Spirit in all is truly able to rejoice.

↓

Joyousness is the armor of those who welcome challenges and tests in the process of growing. Realizing their advancement in body, mind, and Spirit, their cup of joy runs over.

↓

Joyousness is nourished by calm, creative thinking that helps find the right formula for success in what we do.

↓

Joyousness is a ray of sunshine that smiles upon us when we realize that this life is like a passing dream and that we can always do our best if we do not take experiences too seriously.

SUGGESTED AFFIRMATIONS

What I focus on expands. I focus on light, hope, joy, and harmony.

I can experience anything I decide to.
I choose to experience optimism and joy.

Life is but a dream. I do not take it too seriously.

I am making memories every day.
I concentrate on happy memories.

I am part of the Light of Joy;
No darkness can cover my glow.
I can fly as high as an eagle
In the sky of my mind.

Calmness or Restlessness

CENTER OF CALM

One of the best tests for knowing if we are evolving Godward is to examine our degree of calmness. The pure essence of Spirit resides in the inner stillness beyond all vibratory motion, or in the quiet sanctuary of the soul. One who is close to God is steeped in calmness, an inner experience that fills us with peace and security. Know for certain that if an experience leaves you feeling agitated or restless, it is not from God.

ACTIONS

If you have drawn closer to the Supreme Changeless Calm, then the ups and downs of this world of change do not affect you. In that calm state of consciousness it is possible to perform and enjoy what you do with concentration and efficiency.

Sincerely offering the results of all your actions to the Supreme Employer results in calmness. If a person feels attached to the outcome of his actions, then he is serving the ego and will feel anxiety about success or failure and will not be able to be calm and joyous.

POSSESSIONS

We can maintain a healthy, refreshing state of poise if we enjoy the beauty and marvels of creation without trying to possess them. If we carry out all our responsibilities realizing that all creation's gifts are given to use rather than own, then there will be a feeling of attunement with little attachment to things. If we feel attached to possessions, then thoughts of protecting or making them secure will tend to result in a state of disquiet. If we can simplify our lives and own only what we need instead of wanting endless things all the time, then the breeze of calmness will cool us.

SENSATIONS

A focussed and disciplined mind can disconnect itself from the influence of sensations at will, impartially viewing them as being

either harmonious or inharmonious. A controlled mind physically or mentally removes all disturbing vibrations without being affected by them. Gandhi, for example, underwent an operation in full consciousness while talking to friends.

An uncontrolled or undisciplined mind is affected and disturbed by every change. If a sensation is harmonious and affords pleasure, then it becomes attached to that state. If the sensation is inharmonious and pain is experienced, then dislikes are formed. If discrimination and self-control are not developed, then the emotions will follow the troughs and crests of sensations. The constant pursuing of likes and the avoidance of dislikes produces a restless, moody life. The calm master is in control—not controlled by the fluctuating waves of life's changes.

CHART STUDY: CALMNESS OR RESTLESSNESS

"Be still and know that I am God" is the essence of the following chart. If we are free from restlessness or agitation in body and mind, then we shall rest in our own inner calm.

If an experience is creating waves in the lake of your inner being, analyze the reasons why and remove the cause.

CALMNESS OR RESTLESSNESS

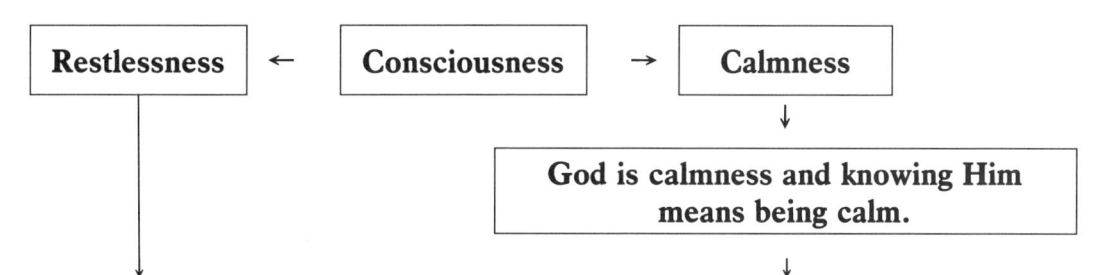

Restlessness ← **Consciousness** → **Calmness**

↓

God is calmness and knowing Him means being calm.

↓ (Restlessness)

Restlessness comes as a result of noting and identifying with change in a changing world.

↓ (Calmness)

Behold the one changeless Light behind all the changing faces of the universe. Anchor yourself in that and there is no reason to be affected by temporal change.

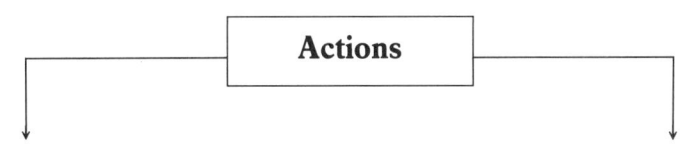

Actions

Working only for our own selfish ends will make us impatient and depressed by failure or overly elated by success. The anticipation and anxiety that result from concentrating on the outcome of our actions is a waste of mental and emotional energy that leaves us exhausted and disappointed and does not help our efforts.

With awareness of the changeless soul within, we can perform our duties with concentration and efficiency. We need not concern ourselves with the outcome of actions or cater to any feelings of personal attachment to them. If we give our work to the Divine Plan, through inner calmness we become united to the changeless Spirit who performs all actions in creation from a centre of infinite calm.

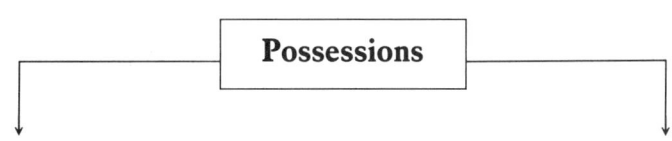

Possessions

The mind becomes restless when it is concerned with worries of possessions, especially if one lives beyond one's means. Thoughts of defending them and meeting payments preoccupy the mind with restlessness.

Enjoy the gifts of the Creator, but do not be so wrapped up in them that you have no time for God. Do not let possessions possess you. Be possessed by God and His love. Look after your responsibility, knowing where you can best put your talents to work to bring in the New Age, for this will bring you peace and satisfaction.

Sensations

The fickle mind that concentrates on like and dislikes never knows inner calmness. If we feel that a certain sensation will make us happy and other sensations will make us unhappy, then there will be no end to our troubles. We will always be affected and irritated by the dualities of life—heat and cold, pleasure and pain, health and sickness, etc. We will never relax and accept whatever is.

The powerful mind views any sensation impartially as being harmonious to the body. If it is harmful, it can be avoided, if it is only unpleasant we can develop tolerance so we are not disturbed by every little change that comes along.

SUGGESTED AFFIRMATIONS

>I am not blown about by the emotions around me;
>I bring stillness and inner calm to every situation.
>
>In my center is a still pond of peace;
>The winds of emotions cannot reach there to ruffle it.
>
>I am at peace in a divinely ordered universe.
>I live from a centre of infinite calm.
>
>Peace shows in my movements;
>Peace is in my voice and eyes.
>Peace is the altar of my Spirit,
>For I am a child of God.

Gossip, Judgment, and Criticism

DESTRUCTIVE ATTITUDES

Gossip, judgment, and criticism are self-defeating practices. The one indulging in them puts out inharmonious vibrations that will eventually come back to him or her. Through the magnetism of association we attract the very thing we condemn. What we focus on is what we experience.

Most of us do not realize that we have within ourselves any fault that bothers us in others. It seems to be human nature to point the finger at someone else in an unconscious attempt to disguise our own flaws. A person with a superiority complex usually puts this face to the world and often condemns others because of his or her own deep-seated insecurities, in this way building himself up to hide his own weaknesses. If the sword of criticism is turned and cuts through their mask, these people often revolt at even the mildest rebuke. Remember that when we point the finger of criticism at someone else, three fingers may be pointed back at us. Others are quick to see what we may not realize about ourselves.

Gossip and destructive criticism have never helped or uplifted anyone. They only create anger, deeper insecurities, and despair. No one likes to be criticized or reminded of shortcomings. Usually, they are already aware of them and are struggling to overcome them. We take ourselves down when we demean anyone else.

CONSTRUCTIVE ATTITUDES

Each of us is at his own stage of evolution and has to go through his own experiences in order to grow. We are all unique and need different lessons at different stages of our development. Our Creator is the only one that knows where we have been and where we are going. Supreme Intelligence is aware of each soul's need and the next step in its unfoldment. No one else has the understanding or the right to assume this responsibility for another.

If you have a desire to help others, then praise their positive qualities. Everyone needs reassurance and support. Putting the spotlight

on another's virtues is the best way to help him or her expand them and overcome weaknesses.

A sincere effort to develop one's own best nature will do far more for others than a critical attitude ever will. By the inspiration of your loving example individuals will tend to be inspired to work on their own growth. If others are drawn to you because of your uplifting influence and seek your guidance, then sincerely help them, but only when asked, and still without criticism.

CHART STUDY: GOSSIP, JUDGMENT, AND CRITICISM

If you find you have the inclination to judge others and to criticize, then review the following study chart. Discover the underlying reasons for your criticism and then look for the Constructive Remedies that can help you become a positive influence instead of a destructive one.

GOSSIP, JUDGMENT, AND CRITICISM

Destructive Tendencies

Gossip and judgment are mankind's most destructive habits. He who indulges in this pastime is often in error himself. By dwelling on it in others we draw attention to ourselves.

Gossip and criticism have never helped anyone overcome faults. They only discourage and cause resentment and despair.

Gossiping people find it easy to talk about the faults of others but cannot stand having their own faults exposed even mildly.

Gossip and destructive criticism are a defense mechanism by which people try to forget and hide their own faults under the mask of a superior attitude. They bolster themselves by putting down others. This seldom fools anyone.

Gossiping about the weaknesses of others causes one to focus on negative characteristics and stimulates one's own bad habits. Quite often people like to gossip about some situation and are attracted to it because either consciously or subconsciously they have that same fault or desire to behave in that way themselves.

Constructive Remedies

"Judge not that ye be not judged."* "He that is without sin among you, let him cast the first stone."†

How can I know what is in another's conscience or soul? And so how can I judge or criticize him?

Let us look at our own motives when tempted to criticize or judge someone else.

Hear, speak, think, and feel no evil. Keep your attention on the beauty of each soul and praise positive qualities. They will then multiply.

Look into yourself instead of gossiping and criticizing others. Spend your time profitably by finding your own shortcomings and changing them. People will then be helped and stimulated to change by your uplifting example.

Condemn no one. Show forgiveness, understanding and kindness. Very often people err because they do not realize how they hurt themselves by not following laws of right living. Condemnation brings despair to them and discredit to you and makes changing even harder for them and you.

Sympathize with others and feel compassion for them as you would feel for yourself. By this attitude you will feel and understand the problems of others and can offer helpful suggestions if asked.

* Matthew 7:1
† John 8:7

SUGGESTED AFFIRMATIONS

> I cannot know what's in another's heart
> So I will accept each person as he is.
>
> When I judge another by my standards
> I shut the door to learning another point of view.
>
> Other people are mirrors in which I see myself.
>
> As I dislike being condemned,
> I will not condemn others;
> As I appreciate kindness from others,
> I will express kindness to all.
>
> I know that God loves and does not judge me;
> He offers loving support.
> So will I love and encourage my neighbor
> In gratitude for the help I receive.

Jealousy and Envy

Jealousy or Unconditional Love

A display of jealousy is not an indication of love or admiration for someone but is an expression of our own hurt and self-concern. A person who indulges in this emotion usually uses it in order to bind and manipulate another. If it proves unsuccessful, then anger, hatred, or the tendency to indulge in self-pity usually develops.

Pure, unconditional love seeks the highest fulfillment and happiness for the beloved. When we love another without expectations, we cannot be disappointed. A person who has this state of consciousness can put the needs of others before his or her own. If a partner achieves success, the one who truly loves is not threatened by it, but instead the joy is magnified. If a partner is attracted to someone else, that is the time to show our generosity and charming, positive qualities. These are more likely to bring a partner back than anger, accusation, or arousing guilt.

Unfaithfulness in a Relationship

If someone is unfaithful, we have been conditioned to feel hurt, but nothing is gained from indulging in jealousy and envy. If we love and respect ourselves, we do not see the problem as demeaning us but as a cry for help. From a centre of kindness and understanding we can express how we feel, then let it be. Any expression of jealousy, anger, or self-righteousness will only widen the gap in a relationship.

If you can maintain a centre of calm understanding and analyze the situation clearly, you will probably find there is something in your own character that has contributed to this situation. If there is, come to terms with the problem and remove it from your life. Then strengthen the power of your magnetism by making yourself shine with kindness and understanding.

Unfaithfulness does not need to be the end of a relationship; it is only a problem in it.

This is also true of other situations that produce conflicts in a marriage. Work with sincerity and love to solve these differences. You will probably be able to make the relationship whole and better than it was before.

If after sincere, repeated efforts unwanted behaviour patterns continue to manifest and grow, then it is often best to part and go separate ways. Better to leave one another as friends who sincerely tried their best than as rivals or enemies.

Jealousy of Others' Excellence

If you admire the genius of another and find yourself feeling envious of his or her talent, this can be a helpful spur to use your own initiative and abilities to become a genius as well. If you indulge in jealousy and tie up your creative energy with a negative emotion, this will be destructive. It is also undesirable to compare one's self to another. See the best in great men and women and then concentrate on developing your own special attributes. Each of us has his own strengths; we are not meant to be copies of someone else, no matter how successful they seem to be.

Chart Study: Jealousy

If jealousy has been one of your problems, then take time to have a long look at your life to determine the underlying cause. Find the Creative Thought Remedies below that can uplift and aid you in harmonizing your life.

JEALOUSY AND ENVY

Jealousy in a Relationship

Destructive Jealousy

Jealousy is a selfish feeling and is not a proof of love for someone else. It centers on concern for only one's own feelings.

Jealousy is a possessive attitude that tries to manipulate, confine, and control others for one's own purposes.

Jealousy is destructive. It leads to hatred for the one that was originally loved and stimulates negative emotional reactions in both parties.

Jealousy tends to lead to vengefulness, which harms the vindictive person most of all.

Responses to Replace or to Meet Jealousy or Envy

Feelings of envy or jealousy can be a stimulus to understanding the plight of a loved one or how our actions may be hurting him or her.

If a loved one is unfaithful to your trust, express how you feel in kindness and calm understanding. After giving this information say no more; do not demand or try to reform him with a self-righteous attitude. Avoid pushing him further away from you or into negative emotions by anger or by accusing.

Manifest greater love and concern. Be extra forgiving and cheerful, making sure that your behaviour is the very finest. The only way to win back love is by knowing your own worth and showing loving concern.

If you find that you have done all you can in sincerity and love and the relationship has not healed itself, then it is usually best to part ways in peace.

Jealousy or Envy of Others

Jealousy or envy is detrimental if one's creative energy is wasted in being envious of the success of others instead of applying that initiative to attain personal success.

Jealousy is harmful if we begin to compare ourselves with others and desire what they have instead of taking stock of our own gifts and talents and developing our own unique gifts.

Constructive envy of someone's success is beneficial if it stimulates one's intelligence and will to achieve more than before.

Envy of others' good qualities is helpful if it inspires us to listen to their wisdom so we may gain insights and higher ideals that we can use in perfecting our own creative originality.

SUGGESTED AFFIRMATIONS

**God loves each of His children equally;
I have no need to envy anyone else.**

**I am proud of who and what I am;
I hold no one in bondage to me.**

**I am discovering my own uniqueness and worth;
I have no need to be like someone else.**

**A loving attitude creates nearness;
A jealous disposition drives others away.
I transmute feelings of jealousy
Into calm understanding and support.**

**Envy of others' excellence demeans my own abilities and talents.
I gather my own abilities and attributes to bring forth my own excellence.**

Flattery and Criticism

The Dual Nature of Flattery and Criticism

Most people find flattery pleasurable and criticism painful. With a new perspective we can experience flattery and criticism without either pleasure or pain. Criticism need not be painful if we look at it as an opportunity to grow. If the accusations are true or even partly true, an accepting attitude hastens our evolution as we change our weaknesses so as to manifest positive soul qualities. If criticisms are unjustified, we can merely hear them and let them go. If we just say "I hear you" and no more, we win.

Criticism is painful if we allow a tender ego to upset us and make us strike back or put up emotional defences. The impulsive reaction to strike out is usually accompanied by such downgrading statements as "How dare you say this to me—who do you think you are?" If violent, explosive behaviour is returned for criticism, then it can be extremely painful if it leads to a black eye or a lawsuit. Why is it that we take seriously critical or demeaning or even insulting remarks from some person whose opinion is not respected? If we do not think they have good judgment, we might listen to their advice and go our way. Why, if their judgment is not respected or admired, be ruffled if they tell us their opinion of us? They do have a right to their views, but we do not need to give them any power over us.

If the person is saying this to get us to react, why should we let him or her manipulate us and spoil our calm? The best answer is "I hear you," and then go calmly on. That will have a far greater impact than anger, which only calls forth more of the same—making the other person feel right, while neither of you feels good.

When people are constructively criticized, they seldom accept the gift but try instead to justify their positions. Some even try to make a wrong look right. Good examples of emotional defence statements contain the word *but*. "But you don't understand," or "What you say is true, but . . ." There are also those

who are so sensitive to criticism that they feel devastated by the slightest reprimand and retreat within and sulk, or run away hurt.

Flattery is useful if praise is used as encouragement to continue strengthening our positive qualities and developing new ones. Flattery can be painful if we allow it to puff up our pride and thus prevent us from seeing and working with our shortcomings. Flattery is also embarrassing if we find we have been taken advantage of or manipulated and have paid a price.

Chart Study: Flattery and Criticism

Studying this chart can help you understand the dual nature of flattery and criticism. When you learn how these qualities can constructively serve you, then you can use their power in your ever-expanding evolution.

FLATTERY AND CRITICISM

Flattery and Criticism
↓

Flattering words from others linked with our own foolish pride prevent us from learning to know our real spiritual and psychological nature.

↓

People who give false praise are not friends, for they usually do so to manipulate others for their own gain.

↓

We can lose money, time, health, and even character from listening to sweet flattery and patting our own backs.

Harsh Criticism from Others
↓

Usually our first reaction when receiving destructive criticism is to put up emotional defences and to strike back.

↓

The insecure ego rebels and immediately finds fault with the criticizing person and inwardly feels, "How dare you—who do you think you are?"

↓

This attitude can lead to angry words and, in some cases, violence. It solves nothing and does no good. It is an opportunity lost.

How to Handle Criticism and Flattery
↓

Stand apart from yourself and see yourself through the eyes of the person criticizing or flattering you.

↓

If the criticism or flattery is justified, thank them for their concern and treat it as a gift. If the accusation is false, inwardly bless them that they may understand, and quietly know the strength of your own position.

Accepting Constructive Flattery and Criticism
↓

If someone notices and mentions a good quality, acknowledge it in yourself.

It is good to listen to and accept these gifts from others that help us become aware of bad habits—and so be better able to develop more positive qualities.

↓

Be ready to apologize if necessary when you see the criticism is true and your attitude or actions have been hurtful. We have been put on this earth to purify ourselves, so willingly accept any true criticism that helps you move towards God.

↓

Too often we put ourselves down with invalid beliefs. When we have accepted ourselves as we are and come to know ourselves, then we can use this knowledge to evaluate what others say and profit by it or let it go by.

↓

Your critic is usually yourself. Listen to your conscience and it will guide you during each step on the path of life.

Suggested Affirmations

Criticism does not devastate me;
Flattery cannot go to my head.
I accept the truth wherever it is spoken
And act on it for my own development.

I am what I am before God and universal justice;
Praise does not make me better, nor blame worse.
I continue striving for my highest evolution,
Looking on praise and blame as if they were one.

I am confident in my own strengths and talents;
Others cannot affect me.
Criticism is a statement about the speaker;
I listen for the grain of truth.

Other people are mirrors in which I see myself.

Part Three

VIRTUES

Mankind's True State of Being
Is One of Virtue.

Self-Love

UNCONDITIONAL LOVE

When one's relationship with his or her self is right, then one's relationship with others will be right. When one's relationship with others is right, one's relationship to God will be right.

A soul that is filled with the Love of God and self-love knows that he can give unconditional love, which is what God is, and that God, as love, is seeking expression through him or her. As we grow into this state, we learn the joy of giving love unconditionally without any expectation of return. Love freely given without any expectation or desire to possess or manipulate others lifts us above the disappointment most of us feel when what we expect in return for our love is not given. The way of the world is to give love with strings attached: "I'll love you if . . ." which is not true love at all.

IN LOVE WITH LOVE

Love is its own reward. When you love you realize that you are in love with love. The love of God emanating from your own heart becomes the object of love. One who is complete and satisfied because of the love coming from within himself has no need to experience it from without. Being saturated with love, he or she can give it freely to others.

If love is received in return, one accepts it joyously and offers it at the feet of the Divine. If one receives persecution or ridicule in return, the sensitive heart may be temporarily hurt but realizes it is lack of understanding in the heart of the other and continues to give love for the welfare of all.

LOVING OTHERS

If you meditate deeply enough to feel the presence of God, you will spontaneously love God and His creation. Saint Teresa of Avila tells us that it is often difficult to know if we love God, but we can certainly know if we are loving others. If one gives to others unconditionally, "Loving one's neighbor as one's self" without expectation of return, then one will eventually find the God of Love in his or her heart. In that love there is no need or want; only satisfaction and joy.

CHART STUDY: SELF-LOVE

Absorb the healing thoughts from this chart and cherish in your heart the unconditional love of God, your love for yourself as a child of God, and the joy of giving love to others.

SELF-LOVE

I now realize that I am inwardly beautiful, loved unconditionally by the Creator of the universe.

↓

Not only am I loved by God who is love itself, but that love is within me, and I can express it.

↓

I can love myself as God loves me and let go of foolish feelings of not being a good person in my own right.

↓

I am glad to be me, am proud of being me, and will show that me to the world.

↓

When my relationship is right with me, then it will be right with God and everyone else.

↓

I can love others as they are, without the need to protect, possess, and manipulate to fulfill my expectations or need for acceptance.

↓

I realize others are going through what they need to go through and have a right to be who and where they are, as I have the same right. I can accept them just as they are.

My concern now is to give love without expectation of return.

↓

If I receive love in return, I enjoy it but I no longer have a desperate need to receive it.

↓

If I receive any negativity in return for my love, I will know that it has nothing to do with me. It is because the other person is not in tune with the beauty of his own soul and so cannot see beauty in me.

Love beams from the face of people who are secure in self-love.

↓

Love acts as a magnet, and others naturally and spontaneously respond.

Suggested Affirmations

I can only love and value others
When I love and value myself.

I no longer need love so desperately
That I have to question and try those I love.

I love myself as God loves me—unconditionally.

I hold myself in the highest regard.

I know my own worth, I am secure in God's love.
I no longer expect rejection from others.

I was created out of love;
The Creator's love is always with me
I can work on my imperfections
And still truly love my uniqueness and beauty.

Success Pointers

The entire cosmos was created with the thought and will of the Creator. The ideas of Spirit were projected outward and there was light. As free-born children of the Supreme Architect, we can use our gifts of thought and will to create our own universe.

Success thoughts, if sincere and persistent, activate the intelligent etheric vibrations, and the universal vibratory laws of the cosmos respond to produce the desired result. The positive, successful mind acts as a magnet and draws to itself the necessary conditions and materials required for success. If one then employs one's will-power to coordinate the acquired materials and circumstances, then the desired goal will be materialized.

Review the following Creative Thought Statements. Find the ones you feel moved to repeat until your life draws success and prosperity.

SUCCESS STATEMENTS

- Success is achieved by asking Spirit to guide you to the occupation that will help you work out your salvation and also serve God and humanity.

- Success is found through choosing the vocation you feel inwardly directed to. If in doubt, choose one that is in accord with your desires and talents, paying enough to meet your responsibilities.

- Success is aided by asking for guidance from God before beginning each task and then offering the work to Him in the service of mankind.

- Success is found through realizing you are a child of God, heir to your share of the cosmos. Everything in the universe is already yours; therefore ask from the Heavenly Father for your rightful share.

- Success is achieved by knowing that you are a son/daughter of God and deserve nothing but the highest and the best.

- Success is found through serving others. Include the success of others in the pursuit of your own prosperity, for all are the children of God, and their success amplifies your own.

- Success is achieved by working from a centre of calmness.

- Success is found through starting with a small project and persisting until it is completed. As soon as confidence grows, then move on to something more difficult.

- Success is achieved by developing your mental efficiency so that you may acquire whatever you need when you put your mind to it.

- Success is found through concentrating on one thing at a time—not scattering energies, but keeping them single-pointedly on the task before you.

- Success is achieved by not worrying about the success of your work but concentrating fully on the present moment. If you are working for God, then you can leave the results in His hands.

- Success is realized through being creative and original in your ideals and work.

- Success lies in doing little things well.

- Success is found through having enthusiasm about whatever you are doing. Nothing kills success more quickly than indifference or boredom.

- Success is achieved by consistent devotion to your work, with steady efforts to do better.

- Success is realized through patience. Even when you feel you are not advancing, keep the vision of success uppermost in your mind.

- Success is achieved by remembering that all good workers experience obstacles. When problems come, that is the time to give superhuman effort.

- Success is found through hard work. The willingness to work is more important than creative ability. Through this attitude anyone can acquire abilities in whatever field he chooses and advance more than those who have abilities but avoid the work.

- Success comes from not being content with one's achievements. There is always more to learn and accomplish.

- Success is found through viewing a failure as a stimulus to succeed, and a success as a stimulus to achieve more.

- Success comes by moulding your own destiny and not looking to some outward source to do it for you. Opportunities come in life because we have created them.

- Success is found through realizing that there is no task that cannot be accomplished. If you feel that you cannot do something, you are under a delusion. You have divine will with limitless power within!

- Success is aided by using good judgment when making decisions and by seeking the advice of experts when you are not sure.

- Success is realized through being economical and living within your means.

- Success lies in living a balanced life physically, mentally, and spiritually.

SUGGESTED AFFIRMATIONS

> I am secure in myself and move with confidence,
> Knowing that success will crown my efforts.
>
> I deserve nothing but the highest and best.
>
> Each step on the path, each experience,
> Moves me closer to my goal of fulfillment.
>
> Whatever comes into my experience
> I use positively to bring me success.
>
> My Heavenly Father owns the universe.
> I am attuned to a path of ever greater abundance,
> prosperity, achievement, and creativity.
>
> I have infinite potential;
> I can be anything I decide I want to be.
>
> I concentrate on one thought at a time;
> I engage my whole being in one action at a time.
> Success depends on being single-pointed;
> Single-pointed is what I am.
>
> Lord, Thou art everything everywhere;
> I am made in Thine Image.
> All that is Thine is mine;
> All success and prosperity are therefore mine.

Lasting Happiness

Each of us is a threefold being, having a body, a mind, and a soul. To be ideally happy, we need to learn to balance our material, mental, and spiritual lives.

HAPPINESS ON THE MATERIAL PLANE OF EXISTENCE

Claim a Divine Son's or Daughter's Share

In order to have a prosperous life we need to acquire at will the basic material necessities of food, shelter, and clothing. In order to do this, we first need to establish our oneness with God, then claim a divine son's or daughter's share. God is the owner of the universe; everything has been created by Him. We are His children, heirs to the kingdom of Spirit. We are not beggars but sons and daughters of God; therefore we can confidently ask from Him our share. After claiming your divine birthright it is essential to remember that God helps those who help themselves. Employ all your God-given abilities and put your will into action to work for your goals, and the power of Spirit will aid you.

Work for the Success of Others

If we would be happy, it is important to include the success of others in the pursuit of our own prosperity. Remember that *all* are children of God. The ideal is to give as we have received—to do unto others as we would have them do to us. If we seek prosperity for others, they will in turn give success to us. By helping others, even if we spend our last nickel to help suffering humanity, the great Father will repay us a thousandfold. This is spiritual law.

Life of Simplicity

Happiness is found in living a life of simplicity. The expression "plain living and high thinking" is a good one to add to your life's

vocabulary. Satisfy real needs but not endless whims or wants. It is a waste of talent and time to pursue endless desires and to acquire unnecessary things, for we will then be hounded by worries of possessions and of losing constantly fleeting satisfactions. If you observe people who spend their time pursuing unnecessary material things, you will see they spend their lives protecting and worrying about the things they have and being frustrated about the things they do not have. Avoid cluttering your life with unnecessary material pursuits so that you can expend your energies on higher, permanently rewarding things.

ENVIRONMENT

If happiness is your goal, remember that the environment in which you place yourself and the company you keep have definite influences on your behaviour. These influential forces are often greater than will-power. If we mix with fun-loving people, we will be carried along in the warmth of their merriment. Associating with criminals, even for a short period of time, will tend to start us doing life-diminishing things. Seek the company of successful people. Too many people's thoughts and actions are dominated by the environment they live in and the company they keep. Not having strong inner convictions, they follow sheeplike the social ways of the world. If we introspect deeply and find out what we want in life, we will benefit by associating with people who manifest these tendencies.

HEALTH MAINTENANCE

If you have a healthy body, firm and fit, then it is much easier to be happy. Saint Francis, who was blind and racked with a diseased body, still maintained the inner joy of God, but until we have reached his state it must be remembered that the body does affect the mind and the emotions. Follow a simple, natural, balanced diet. Avoid filling the body with heavy animal products, starches, and sweets. These clog the system and cause restlessness and discomfort. It is very difficult to maintain a joyous attitude when one's body and mind are agitated by stimulants and rich foods. Overeating leads to many health problems; constipation, for example, is one of the worst enemies of happiness and well-being.

It is important to get plenty of exercise in the fresh air. Whenever possible it is beneficial to take in the sun's healing rays to help the body remove toxins. The sun is a great healer and vitalizer. Bacteria can not survive in the sun's purifying rays.

CHOOSING A VOCATION

One's life vocation needs to be in accordance with one's innate soul nature so that each of us can manifest his or her unique and special attributes. The proper vocation allows our positive qualities to blossom and will give us the opportunity to grow and perfect ourselves. Never should work be undertaken only for acquiring money. The main focus should be harmonious with our spiritual nature, working for the betterment of life on earth. Work that is creative and in a spirit of service to God and humanity will bring the most satisfaction. If our attitudes and motives are right, then the service performed will be a benefit to ourselves as well as to God and humankind.

Renunciation

Renunciation is the art of overcoming by giving up the things that will eventually make us unhappy. It opens the door to happiness as it teaches us to turn attention from illusive sense pleasures to the ever-new joy of the soul life within. If we live a life of indulgence, catering to the sense of sight, smell, taste, hearing, and touch, then we eventually become satiated and bored. Living on the sense plane eventually smothers the fine sensitivity that alone can lead to happiness. The secret is to be so filled with inner joy that we spiritualize our material life. In this way we can enjoy simple pleasures, such as eating wholesome food or socializing with friends, without painful attachments or results. If we can cultivate this attitude, then when something in this fleeting material world is taken from us, we shall not be crushed. Penniless we come into this world, and penniless is the way we will go out. It is wise, then, to cultivate nonmaterial satisfactions. We can prepare ourselves for the spiritual life by giving our attention to that which lives beyond the grave—the life of soul.

HAPPINESS ON THE MENTAL PLANE OF EXISTENCE

Concentration

In the mental world we can dowse for happiness with the rod of concentration. With a focussed, efficient mind the vast empire of creativity will be able to flow through our being, inspiring all. When we awaken mental qualities of willingness, determination, and persistance we will be able to initiate and bring to fruition accomplishments in all aspects of life. As we become more and more proficient, an inner confidence develops. By aligning ourselves with the strength and beauty of the intuitive soul within, we are able to solve problems and find joyous solutions to all our inquiries. We are able to remove negative, destructive habits from our life and manifest positive ones that bring success and contentment.

Positive Thinking

Happiness is a product of positive thinking and affirmations. The power of the mind is inexhaustible, and if we keep our thoughts, will, and actions centred on one thing, then we will bring that thing into manifestation. When we concentrate on one idea we generate a field of attraction that draws into its radius the thing being affirmed. If we can materialize the things we need by the power of our thoughts, then success and happiness will come so long as we make sure that what we are affirming is in tune with what is for the best good of all.

Attitude of Joy

Happiness is a state of mind. Joy is attained by developing an attitude of unshakable inner happiness despite problems, trials, difficulties, or failures that may come into one's life. In all circumstances we can realize that these situations have been created by our choices and have come to teach us certain lessons, that we may grow. If we do not judge it to be good or bad but look beyond it to its resolution, then we can smile even in adversity.

When we are working to better ourselves and ask the aid of Spirit, nothing happens to us by coincidence. The Divine Plan is that we evolve and perfect ourselves. If we realize this, we shall see that life is helping us unfold and giving us opportunities to use and develop our unique abilities.

Visualization and Imagination

In the realm of visualization and imagination we can be whatever we wish to be and as happy as we want to be. We are all actors on the stage of life, and by using visualization and imagination we can consciously play whatever role we wish. Through our best thoughts we can see ourselves joyously removing the suffering of mankind by our conquering love. We can create a utopia that reigns supreme in our mental sky, where all is beauty and perfection. Visualizations are powerful, and a picture of heaven on earth will aid in making this a tangible reality for all. On a personal level, visualizations have great power in bringing to us what we need or want.

Evenmindedness

The three-dimensional world we live in is a world of relativity. The dualities of positive and negative, heat and cold, light and shadow, joy and sorrow, success and failure, pleasure and pain are always with us. We have need to control our minds so as to be evenminded in all these dualities, lest we travel like a jeep on a bumpy road, going up and down, fluctuating from one mood to the next, always in a state of inconsistency. The ability to be evenminded in all circumstances is the buffer that absorbs the shocks of life, making the journey a joyous, smooth one. Observe people who do not introspect to control their minds and emotions. They swing from one extreme to the other, not understanding why. They often become physical, mental, emotional, or nervous wrecks.

Likes and Dislikes

One of the most effective ways to destroy happiness is to form strong likes and dislikes. Through identification and attachment we then feel that a certain situation or object can make us happy or unhappy. When that something is taken away from us or does not arrive as expected, we feel we cannot be happy. If we strongly dislike something, the moment that object or circumstance comes into the radius of our consciousness we will identify with being unhappy because of it.

This applies to pleasure and pain since we tend to identify happiness with pleasure and discomfort with pain. Pain, however, can be a friend that shows us that we are doing something wrong. It gives us a warning that we must change our ways and actions if we wish to be healthy. We also tend to identify happiness with success and sorrow with failure. Ultimately if failure is viewed in the proper spirit, we can imagine it as an archangel that is spurring us on to greater efforts and hence greater achievements.

It is sensible to rise above the dualities of life and leave behind these vacillating whims, moods, and unfulfilling habits. If the waters of evenmindedness are the dominant undercurrent in your stream of life, they will be a great shock-absorber and an aid in transcending the annoyances and uncertainties of everyday living.

HAPPINESS ON THE SPIRITUAL PLANE OF EXISTENCE

Union of the Soul and Spirit: Spiritual Marriage

The source of all joy is God. When we go to the Source to receive our inspiration, then the whole fountain of joy showers its blessings on us. Meditation is the vehicle that takes us to the place within ourselves where we can be absorbed in the ever-new unchanging bliss of God. As we experience this state of fulfillment we will realize that we are not just a body but a soul made in the joyous Image of Spirit.

There is no greater happiness than that which is experienced in the union of soul with Spirit. In the spiritual marriage the soul is emancipated and gloriously fulfilled. The highest spiritual law finds fulfillment: "Thou shalt love the Lord thy God with all thy heart, soul, mind and strength." When we love and give ourselves completely we feel the deepest joy. By merging all one's love, concentration, and energy in oneness with God, the purest of all joys enters the heart.

Practicing the Presence of God

Practicing the presence of God as a near and dearest friend brings happiness. We all need the warmth of a close companion, a dear one by our side, someone who understands us no matter what we do. When we make that someone God, Christ, Krishna, or whomever we feel devoted to, joy will fill the cup of our life. The Divine is ever ready to walk with us, talk with us, and tell us that we are His own. Conversation with God is the language of your soul. You can share with Him all your desires and fears. As you draw closer and closer to Him in a friendly, intimate way, making Him one of the family, He will shower on you His eternal blessing.

Faith in God's Will

When you learn to see God everywhere in everything and everyone, happiness springs from the immensity of His love. He knows what is best for us. If our desire is to do His Will, we shall see His hidden hand guiding us in all phases of life, for His Will is what is for our best good. When we pray to do the Will of God we must remember that He may be striving to teach us what we need to learn and not necessarily what we want to learn. The Divine Guiding Hand will work through all experiences and through others if we are sincere in wanting to grow in Him, taking everything as it comes and working it through.

Growth in God means to become happier within ourselves. If there is some broken link in the chain of our happiness, then that is the lesson we now need to learn. To realize our oneness with God means that we know unconditional joy. God will always test the weakest link in the chain of our qualities, and He will test it again and again until we have eliminated the weakness. Spirit is constantly trying to protect us from ourselves, for very often the greatest enemy of our own happiness is ourselves. Have faith that God's Love is bringing you to a state of perfection.

Qualities of Spirit

To manifest the divine qualities of God is to manifest happiness. We need to express

through every faculty of our being love, peace, joy, wisdom, compassion, tenderness, power, patience, and humility. Introspection, self-control, and unflinching will and determination are necessary to uproot the weeds of pride of family or of race, of prejudice, smugness, hatred, shame, grief, and fear. Clearing the weeds of negativity appears to be a trying task, but if we remember that we are the gardener working for the Master of the universe, we will find it a worthwhile task. Dedicate yourself to help beautify the universe by making your own inner garden a flourishing, productive one. If everyone beautified his or her own garden of consciousness, there would be heaven on earth.

Working for the Divine in Others

When the kingdom of God reigns on earth, joy will be the sun in every heart. His kingdom comes as we strive to help our brothers and sisters in need. Real, lasting happiness is found in making others happy. A kind word, a smile can do much: it can make the day for some lonely heart. A thoughtful deed, an act of kindness can help to change the world. We can all do our part to light the light of smiles to help spread the glow on other faces. You can love God within and love God in others through love in action. Actions performed in a spirit of nonattachment to the fruits or results, free from personal desire and ambition, performed to please God and others, are the ones that bring heaven to earth. The best attitude is to concentrate on joyously working for Spirit, for the glory of God, not for personal gain. It is no use to barter with God, promising to do something if He will fulfill your desire in return. He does not operate in this way. His universe works on cosmic law. If the motive is pure, what we need is given without our asking.

LASTING HAPPINESS

We are threefold beings with bodies, minds, and souls. To be ideally happy we must balance and be progressing in our material, mental, and spiritual lives.

For Material Happiness

- You can claim from your Heavenly Father your divine share. We are made in the Image of God, and our heritage is the universe.
- Find a fulfilling vocation that satisfies your heart's desire and also serves mankind, and your happiness is assured.
- If you selflessly work to please God and advance humanity, other matters will take care of themselves.
- When you include the success of others in the pursuit of your own prosperity your satisfactions are multiplied.
- Through self-control you can overcome the temptation to abuse the senses. With God in your heart it is natural to enjoy the harmless pleasures of life without attachment.
- Associate with uplifting company and peaceful surroundings.
- Follow natural laws and maintain good health.
- Cultivate the ability to acquire material needs whenever necessary without depending on anyone else.
- Live within your means.
- Avoid catering to desires for unnecessary wants or luxuries so you will not be hounded by worries of possessions and fleeting satisfactions.
- Practice plain living and high thinking.

For Mental Happiness

- Happiness is a state of mind. Through effective, directed thinking you can gain unshakable inner happiness. Under all conditions, despite all problems, trials, difficulties, or seeming failures, it is possible to smile.
- Development of the faculties of memory, imagination, reason, and logic are resources that aid inner happiness.
- Seek to intellectually understand the laws of life, then apply constructive attitudes in everyday dealings with others. This prevents conflict and contributes to well-being.
- Through concentrated mental practice you can gain more and more successes in all phases of your life. Self-confidence and happiness are a natural state.
- Awaken the mental strength within that you may victoriously solve problems and change destructive habits into constructive ones.
- Transcend unstable states of likes, dislikes, whims, moods, insecurities, fears, and thoughts of failure. Keep your mind stable and centered on peace and happiness within.
- Through visualization explore the realm of uplifting thoughts and inspiration. In your mind's eye make yourself what you want to be and enjoy your self-created paradise. It will come into being if you believe and persist.
- Be evenminded in a world of change. Be mentally above changeable sensations so that you are not tied to pleasure, pain, heat, cold, etc.

For Spiritual Happiness

- Realization of our oneness with God through meditation leads to being absorbed in the ever-new changeless bliss of God.
- Loving the Lord with heart, soul, mind, and strength brings unity through the spiritual marriage of the soul with the Divine.
- Practising the presence of God as a near and dear friend leads to seeing God everywhere in everything.
- Faith in the immensity of God's love for us and the knowledge that God knows what is best for our lives leaves no room for unhappiness, doubt or turmoil.
- Tuning into the Will of God, then using our own will and activity to help build His kingdom on earth, brings the highest form of happiness.
- Strive to please God and help mankind in all your actions.
- Practice nonattachment to the results of your actions; perform them for God, and leave the results in His hands.
- Find happiness in making others happy.
- Overcome negative qualities and manifest the positive ones of the soul: intuition, love, peace, joy, wisdom, compassion, tenderness, patience, humility, etc.
- Free yourself from emotional desires and attachment to worldly things.
- Learn to intuitively know the answers to all your questions.

SUGGESTED AFFIRMATIONS

My birthright is joy.

I am worthy of happiness.
I have the power to create joy in my life.
I choose to find happiness and joy in everything I do.

I know how to chart my way; the future holds no fear.
I am filled with contentment and joy.

I attract the people, vocation, and experiences that express my Divinity.

I am manifesting my Divine Plan and Purpose
And so am filled with joy.

I balance my living with work, play, and inner devotion;
My reward is harmony and success in all areas of my life.

Secure in God's love,
I am content to work for the coming of peace and brotherhood on earth.

Part Four

RELATIONSHIPS

Those Who Learn to Love Unconditionally
Have Found the Heart of God.

Relationships

POWER OF LOVE

God, the One Spirit, created the universe by projecting a portion of Himself outward. God created the many and is calling the many back unto Himself. Will is the power that projected the universe; love is the magnet that is drawing it back.

Light was the first expression of creation which dispersed into a sea of electrons. Spirit implanted the magnetic force of love in every particle of space. This magnetic love attracted various electrons together to create nebula, then planetary systems. Holy love, manifesting more tangibly, drew various electrons and elements together to create vegetation, the animal kingdom, and finally man. The magnetic pull of love continues its evolution and attracts different people together in various relationships in order to help each other evolve. Love supreme then draws a disciple to the feet of a Master where he or she can learn techniques of emancipation. The final touch of love awakens the heart of the seeker to its oneness with Spirit.

THE PURPOSE OF RELATIONSHIPS

Relationships are an essential part of God's Plan in the evolution of a soul. The soul draws to itself the circumstances and people it needs for its highest development. In all our contacts and communications we are meant to help each other develop the divine qualities of love, peace, kindness, patience, and so on, even though mankind does not usually realize this. The supreme ideal would be that all souls walk hand-in-hand to the One.

Through many lives of interacting with others in various situations we have formed complex personalities. They are interlaced with desires, likes and dislikes, eccentricities, and also developed soul qualities. When two people interact there will be points of harmonious attraction and also obvious differences.

MARRIAGE AND SPIRITUAL LAW

The relationship we shall concentrate on is marriage. In the art of forming and maintaining any close relationship there are important

guidelines of conduct that will allow souls to be drawn closer together in a harmonious unity. Many of the rules that apply to marriage apply to other relationships as well.

Marriage is a creation of Spirit, not man, and functions under the laws of the cosmos. The true marriage of two souls is very sacred in God's eyes. This relationship was created with the purpose of uniting the love of each heart into one love. The Father's desire is that we realize our oneness with Him in the transformation of human love into divine love.

The marriage relationship, once undertaken, is a sacred responsibility. It is not to be based on physical, intellectual, or emotional attraction alone; rather, it is a definite commitment one to the other to manifest our highest and best. This vow needs to be constantly worked on and may require compromises from both partners in order to create the necessary harmony to allow the best inner qualities to manifest in each partner.

COMMUNICATION

Communication between marriage partners is one of the most important single factors in a harmonious marriage. Couples need to put aside a regular time when they can discuss their problems. Open and honest sharing of thoughts, feelings, and needs is necessary if both partners are to feel they are traveling the same path.

Man tends to be reason-oriented; woman tends toward feeling. At times men are too preoccupied and have a difficult time discussing or expressing their feelings. They may show strong emotions concerning their opinions and involvements but are often inhibited in expressing their own personal feelings. This tendency may give a wife the impression that her husband is cold, indifferent, or uncaring toward her. If a woman then nags at her husband, showing agitation or emotion, he is likely to retreat further into his mental world.

Women sometimes find they are caught up emotionally in a situation and find it difficult to think of or listen to their husbands' logic. A husband may think his wife is being totally unreasonable in her accusations or emotional demands.

Each partner needs to try to make a real effort to see the other's point of view. If it is difficult for a man to express his feelings, he needs to compromise and make an honest effort to do so. If it is foreign for a wife to reason a situation out, she needs to make an attempt to listen to, and think in terms of, her husband's reasoning. If each partner makes an honest effort to meet the other half-way, then respect is born. A man can develop the feeling side of his nature and a woman can develop her ability to reason. Through communication each partner can move toward a better balance of reason and feeling and realize that the other truly does care.

If a partner is bothered by a fault in the other, this should be communicated from a state of sincerity, wisdom, and love, free from complaint. It is best to express only how that fault affects one's own feelings. Communication on this level will help each partner to see what causes difficulty and have an opportunity to remedy it. In this supportive environment both partners will grow, and a solid relationship can be established. Too often one of the partners makes all the compromises and the other takes it for granted.

Resentment then builds up in the woman until a real crisis develops, and the other finds it inexplicable. This can be prevented with open communication.

Respect

Everyone is made in the Image of God. Your mate is an incarnation of Spirit with a treasurehouse of divine qualities within. Each of us has been given special gifts, and your partner has qualities that are unique. He or she is God's own and is loved no matter what his or her shortcomings are.

Respect is the foundation of a good relationship, and to keep it alive it is important to keep the eyes of love focussed on your partner's good qualities and not on his or her mistakes. In this world of relativity it is possible to see flaws in even the greatest music or literary compositions. If one gets in the habit of criticizing and looking for faults, and this robs us of the pleasure of the things that are good and inspiring, in the close proximity of the home a partner's flaws will tend to be magnified. Keep the gaze of respect riveted on the special attributes that your partner possesses, the things that drew you together in the first place, and your admiration will cause them to grow.

In order for respect to be maintained both partners must work at building their positive qualities and behaviour skills. It is easy to have a tendency to let ourselves slide after we have convinced our partner of our worthiness as a lifetime investment. The original commitments and ideals that were shared need to be maintained and developed further day by day.

Watch to see that your partner does not feel used or manipulated in order to satisfy your own self-centered desires. Respect his or her needs, and with creative enthusiasm work together for their fulfillment. If your partner is happy and fulfilled, you will feel the same happiness and contentment, so long as you do not violate yourself or deny your own needs.

Sex was created for the purpose of having children as well as for showing love and appreciation for one's partner. Love yearns for oneness, and the sex act gives expression to this oneness in the joining of body, mind, and soul. If sex is used as an expression of lust, then in time self-respect and the respect of one's partner will diminish. If love and its channels of expression are not used for their highest purpose, then love will fade away.

Appreciation

A marriage remains on a firm foundation when each partner feels and shows appreciation for the other. Some men have tremendous appreciation for their mates but find it difficult to convey the feeling to them. Sometimes it is kept inside and not expressed because a man, for example, thinks his wife already knows it or should know it. Usually the wife has her own uncertainties and does *not* know and is yearning to hear some words of appreciation. If either mate has a tendency to complain or criticize, then the partner may certainly get the impression that he or she is not appreciated.

To keep the bond strong, partners need to communicate through words and thoughtful acts that they appreciate their mates. Showing appreciation for even the small, everyday acts that a partner does to serve the other goes a long way toward making a marriage satisfying to both participants.

The Best Relationship

There can be no relationship without problems. If one thinks changing partners will bring happiness and fulfillment, there will be disappointment. The marriage a person is in right now is usually the best marriage unless, of course, there is violence or insurmountable physical, mental, or emotional problems that should not be tolerated in any marriage.

Our karma or vibrational pattern has drawn to us the very person we need to help us grow emotionally and spiritually. Life is a school, and we attract to us the circumstances and individuals we need to learn life's lessons.

If a partner feels that his or her mate is not spiritual or intellectual enough, it should be remembered that the person before you is a soul made in the Image of God. Until you have patiently persevered to show understanding and cooperation in working out all difficulties, and until you have used all resources to bring about a reconciliation or mutual understanding, it is unlikely that you will find lasting happiness with anyone else. We carry our problems with us and will attract the same lessons again until we have dealt with our own inner flaws.

In Love with Love

As the soul grows in love, it cherishes this sacred feeling in the heart. By holding and developing love in the heart, the soul begins to realize that it is in love with love itself. The love that is felt for a husband, wife, child, country, or ideal becomes the object of love. The soul comes to feel and know that it has realized the love of God. The human relationship becomes divine as the presence of Spirit is experienced through it.

The following Creative Relationship Statements can help you grow toward your ideal. Use them as a guide and inspiration in your daily life. Above all, try to live by them so that they become a permanent part of your thinking and character.

A HAPPY RELATIONSHIP

- A satisfying relationship's blueprint is love: a spontaneous gift from the heart.

- A happy relationship is enhanced when the consciousness of both focusses on the heart centre, where love is supreme.

- A successful relationship expands a couple's deep love for one another to include the love of all God's creatures.

- A good relationship develops as each partner feels deepening bonds of harmony in body, mind, and soul with the other.

- A fulfilling relationship is structured to help each partner develop his/her inner qualities. Man's reason tends to be predominant; woman's feelings are usually uppermost. The union of man and woman merges these qualities and helps both to learn and grow.

- A happy relationship's foundation is one where sex is treated with respect, either for the creation of children or as a physical expression of love for the other.

- A satisfying relationship's life-line is trust, where each can discuss his/her feelings and opinions in open communication with understanding and no fear of censure.

- A successful relationship is one that is worked on constantly and is not left to develop by chance.

- A fulfilling relationship is housed in the expression of soul qualities of kindness, patience, self-respect, and love.

- A happy relationship is nourished by an attitude of thoughtfulness for the happiness of one's mate. It includes a willingness to sometimes give up or postpone one's personal desires in order to bring happiness into the other's life.

- A good relationship lives on the plane of high moral standards and ideals.

- A satisfying relationship comes from working in harmony as a unit to achieve similar spiritual ideals and goals.

- A successful relationship excels when each mate is increasingly more considerate of, and helpful to, his/her partner.

- A happy relationship matures through a feeling of friendship and companionship with each other.

- An excellent relationship is enhanced if each partner keeps his bodily temple clean and healthy, develops his mind, and strives to bring his/her best into the marriage.

- A fulfilling relationship revolves around concern for the growth and perfection of one's mate.

- A successful relationship is a constant unfolding of love and understanding.

- A happy relationship results from calmly discussing problems and being willing to compromise without argument.

- A good relationship is focussed on respect for one's mate and his opinions, friends, and interests.

- A worthwhile relationship offers each partner his privacy and independence when it is best for his/her development.

- A satisfying relationship is sheltered if each partner does not discuss personal and family problems with others.

- A successful relationship is enhanced by appreciation and by giving each other the gifts of dignity and loving attention.

- A good relationship is sustained by humour and idealism.

- A happy relationship is perfumed by keeping the romance alive with small gifts, remembrances, and thoughtfulnesses.

- A worthwhile relationship is deepened if each mate respects the other's privacy when he wishes to work, think, or act alone.

- A satisfying relationship is often quickly achieved if each partner willingly takes turns doing the different household chores. No one should be stuck in the kitchen all the time.

- A relationship grows and is sweetened when each partner shares his thoughts and love and appreciation.

- A successful relationship is founded on a spiritual attraction and union with one's soul-mate.

- A satisfying relationship is built around the love of God and the desire of each partner to know Him.

- A fulfilling relationship's cornerstone is praying and meditating daily together to feel the guidance of God and to do His Will. "A family that prays together stays together."

- A happy relationship is rooted in loyalty. Each partner thinks of his mate as God's gift to help in learning to purify love.

ELEMENTS HARMFUL TO A RELATIONSHIP

- Avoid a relationship that is primarily based on material advantage or sex attraction.

- Shun a union where sex is used for sense gratification, where there is promiscuity or overindulgence; it results in disrespect and disgust.

- Realize that it is a misconception that sex is love. Sexual union is love only if practiced as an expression of love.

- Avoid undue suppression of the sex impulse; it will tend to lead to frustration and guilt feelings. Continence is a natural evolution of deeper bonds of soul love, making moderation and self-control a true expression of the inner self. However, if abstinence is practiced without the readiness of both partners, an underlying tension will probably result and give rise to serious problems.

- Weed out the negative qualities of jealousy, anger, inconsiderations, cruelty, discourtesy, crankiness, suspicion, insulting speech or acts, selfishness, and unkind words. If these are used on others, they will eventually come back to us.

- Avoid trying to manipulate one another by using questions, suggestions, demands, threats, bribes, complaints, begging, or arousing guilt feelings to get your own way.

- Realize the shallowness of relating only on the sense level of existence.

- Avoid overfamiliarity, which breeds contempt and revulsion.

- Guard against a tendency to be possessive.

- Be aware that if you stray from ideals and moral standards, you will lose the respect of your mate.

- Avoid insulting or arguing with one another, especially in front of others.

- Be careful never to take advantage of one another nor to take your mate for granted.

- Avoid discussing private elements of your life together with others, no matter how wonderful they are.

SUGGESTED AFFIRMATIONS

    I love my partner as I love myself—unconditionally.

    **In the sharing of peace and love with my partner
I find my fulfillment deepened and expanded.**

    **My mate is a very special person; if difficult,
I hold his (her) exceptional qualities in mind as we work together.**

    **I am making unconditional love my ideal;
I am focussing on all the positives in our marriage.**

    **I realize I have been wrapped up in my own concerns;
I open myself to understanding my partner's problems.**

    **I see I have been hard on my partner's feelings.
My intention now is to respect his/her right to be her-/himself.**

    **I realize that to discuss problems doesn't mean I am a failure;
Instead of showing irritation I will listen to my partner.**

    **I see that when I approach my partner angrily
It shuts the door to communications.
I now wait until I am calm to express my feelings.**

    **From the One Spirit came many souls;
The many are now travelling back to the One.
Each soul I know is a companion
With whom I am travelling back to the One.**

Part Five

BEHAVIOUR SKILLS

To Do What Is Comfortable Is Easy and Gives Limited Results.
To Do What Is Right Is Often More Difficult, but the Rewards Are Greater.

Be Your Real Self

THE INNER AND OUTER SELF

Most people identify with, and focus on, their exterior characteristics. They associate with a name, a body type or complexion, a job or a role that they play in society. The wise who look within see themselves as souls made in the Image of God. In order to be your Real Self you must turn your attention from the outer to the Inner Self.

The Inner Self sees its nature as ever conscious, ever existing, an omnipresent joyous soul. The outer self sees that it has a name, a body with a certain color of eyes belonging to a certain family or job or profession. The Soul Self unites its will with the Will of God and knows that the wisdom and guidance it is experiencing are from the Supreme Intelligence of the universe. The ego self is guided by the limitations of the intellect and emotions and follows the dictates of customs, desires, and influences from others. The Real Self expresses the inner soul qualities of love, peace, and kindness in order to be at its best and to help uplift humanity. The delusive self is often forced to play a role to maintain a concept or image of how it wants to believe it is.

CHART STUDY: BE YOUR REAL SELF

In the following chart we list characteristics of the ego, which operates from an exterior self-image, and the soul's expression of its true nature.

BE YOUR REAL SELF

My Self-Image (Imagined Image)

I am a woman/man, doctor, secretary, teacher, rebel, whatever.

↓ Role Planning for the Future

↓ Energy tied up in anticipation of the future

↓ Nervousness

Depletion of energy and awareness for natural living

Desire to impress society and others ↓

Motive

Manipulate others to gain something.

— To bring a response from others.

↓ To convince others how great I am.

↓ Lead to a fear of failure.

↓ Being troubled by disappointments, fear of what people think and of what they may do.

↓ Role Playing

My actions are controlled. I feel compelled to act differently than I would like.

Demands are placed on me. I respond regardless of whether this is best for me.

There is a compulsion to act out my accepted role.

I manipulate and distort myself to control others or meet their expectations.

I am out of touch with, and do not experience, my true inner feelings.

I am a fragmented being.

Resentment, resistance, and frustration consume me.

My Real Self

I am a free soul made in the Image of God. I am a son/daughter of God, a divinely unique individual.

I have no need for a self-image concept, or an ego telling me what I should and must do.

I am in tune with the energies within myself, others, and my surroundings.

Motive

My actions are in tune with God's Will for me, which is for my own best good and that of others.

I am free to follow the guidance of soul-inspiring wisdom.

I express my highest desires and feelings honestly and directly.

I Express My True Self.

SUGGESTED AFFIRMATIONS

My pure essence is Godlike.

My true nature is my soul nature;
I am eternal light and love.

I am bringing my inner beauty and radiance
Into my outer living and circumstances.

I am leaving behind all my old conceptions of who I am
And manifesting what is deepest and truest in my nature.

I disclaim all the characteristics that others ascribe to me
In favour of being who I really am.

I see that I am more than my appearance and personality traits.
I no longer feel impelled to play roles others have put on me;
I am expressing who I really am—and that is someone special.

When I do what others want or expect so as not to hurt them,
I hurt myself and who I really am because I build resentment.
I now express who I am and want to be kindly and firmly.

Psychological Conflict

THE PULL BETWEEN SOUL AND EGO CONSCIOUSNESS

Life is an ever-flowing stream of choices. With our free will we can indulge in whatever we choose. Using this gift brings with it an unsuspected responsibility, for the choices we make determine what we become. Universal Law cautions us to use our gifts of reason and decision-making to our best advantage, because what we put out will come back to us. There is no escape from the law of karma; its precision is awesome when you come to understand it. Each person reaps what he or she sows even if we cannot always see how it comes back to him or her.

We all have to make choices, and each of us has to bear the consequences of his decisions, much as we may want to put responsibility on someone else. Upon awakening each morning, we have numerous options. We can, for example, decide to stay in bed, get up and meditate, dash out the door to work, or go have breakfast. The first thought of a realized soul is of his devotional practice of prayer and meditation. The worldly man may think of food and of what business appointments he has. Every day is charged with a series of decisions. Too many choices, however, are made automatically because of habits formed in the past.

In this world of relativity or opposites there are two main forces at work on us. Each force is trying to influence us to make decisions in its favour. The magnetic pull of love is the force that is uplifting us Godward, and the opposite force of the ego is trying to hold us in bondage to the senses. The result is an ongoing struggle between soul and ego consciousness. The soul seeks the subtler, refined vibrations of Spirit; the ego seeks the grosser vibrations of material pleasures.

If we constantly make decisions in support of the ego, then we think everything is all right, because we encounter little or no resistance. The one who is in touch with his higher self makes decisions based on a desire to know God and His Will and thus comes in touch

with Supreme Truth and is established in right living. One who is caught between the two forces experiences inner confusion, feeling pulled in different directions at the same time. The only way out of this dilemma is to make a commitment to go with one side or the other.

World of Sensations

The world's attraction tends to be toward an instantaneous but temporary sense of gratification. One who lives in this consciousness seeks these pleasures whenever and wherever possible. The thought of giving up these gratifications is dismaying to the ego. It views denying pleasures now for something that may possibly be acquired in the future as an absurd and futile concept. Worldly people often feel that if they practice self-denial, they will have nothing to live for.

Those living according to the ego follow their natural urges and flow with whatever they dictate. Resisting this flow is considered unnatural and silly. The ego reasons that the main focus of life is to indulge today, never mind the effects it will produce tomorrow. After all, life is short and we only live once, so let's indulge.

Magnetism of Spirit

The inner life offers a more subtle satisfaction and oneness with things of Spirit. In this state of consciousness there is no desire or want, for the soul finds itself complete and content. This is not an empty state of nothingness but includes everything in the universe.

Oneness with Spirit means that everything that God is, we attain. The seeker becomes one with the universe of love, peace, wisdom, and joyous bliss. All the love that has ever been expressed since the beginning of time is beating in that person's own heart. All the energy of the cosmos is coursing through his or her being. Everything there is to know can be known intuitively.

There are no words to describe the joy that a soul feels when reunited with God. It would not change its state of consciousness for all the gold and pleasures of the world. The gratification of the senses cannot compare to even a small touch of this spiritual bliss, and the joy of God is endless. Once this is attained, the soul's only desire is to reach out and help others join in this wonderful state of tranquility.

Inner Confusion

The soul itself intuitively knows that seeking God is its highest good. Consciousness begins to tangibly realize this after it has reaped untold frustration and misery in trying to satisfy itself through the senses. This truth also comes when a person has a spiritual experience and glimpses the great beauty and joy of the presence of God within.

Consciousness that has tasted Divinity knows it cannot be satisfied with anything less. The soul's wish is to seek God, and the ego tries to lead us to play with the things of the flesh.

The contest is always there. Ego, with the aid of the cosmic delusive force, will use whatever method seems to work to keep a soul busy with sense pleasures. God has touched the soul with love and patiently waits for each of us to come home. From time to time He sends his saints to remind us of the greater joy to be found in His eternal realms.

Chart Study: Psychological Conflict

In the following chart we have a picture-diagram of the conflict in the mind. On one side is the call of Spirit and on the other is the voice of temptation. Where the two forces meet there is a conflict of interests that produces a state of inner confusion.

Analyze your thoughts and actions and determine which side you are supporting. If you are content with your allegiance, then march onward. If you are discontent with your present choice, then you can relocate your support.

PSYCHOLOGICAL CONFLICT

Voices of Temptation

Sense pleasures offer instant gratification. Why should I make any resolutions to change?

I would be foolish to live in emptiness and give up my pleasures for something that I may gain spiritually in the future, no matter how beautiful the promise.

I would rather let temptations rule my life than be involved in the struggle between sense pleasures and spiritual growth.

Go ahead and indulge. What does it matter, anyway?

Eat, drink, and be merry for tomorrow you may die.

Inner Confusion

I feel so guilty about my past habits. They seemed okay before, but now they upset me.

Why do I hold on to past habits when I have an inner sense that something is missing—that there is something better than this for me?

When I try to change, I feel torn as pleasures pull me in one direction and inner growth another.

When I tell myself not to do something, it seems as if my will is paralyzed and my whole body is preventing me from changing. I find it difficult to change these invisible bad habits, and I always seem to be under their control.

As soon as I try to concentrate on noble thoughts, negative ones arise. Where do these thoughts come from? They make me feel insecure, and in order to escape them I want to forget the spiritual life and be as involved in the world of pleasure as I can.

Voices of Conscience*

Sense pleasures do not satisfy me. They only cause me to desire more pleasures, which leave me miserable and unhappy.

When I've behaved in old ways I know that I am being untrue to myself. There is something inside me that knows I can be a better, happier person.

I will not regret giving up little pleasures for the joy of the soul. I know it exists, as every scripture confirms it and I see it in the faces of great Masters and experience it as I grow in spiritual awareness myself.

I will exert enough will-power and persistence to overcome limiting, life-quenching habits.

I will look at my destructive habits and patiently weed them out so I can cultivate ones that bring growth, joy, and satisfaction.

I now focus on uplifting concepts and seek calm spiritual people and thus replace my self-defeating ways by focussing my attention on constructive patterns.

I will meditate until I know I am a unique creation who is loved by God and can become one with Him and work and share His Plan.

*The discriminative voice of the soul.

SUGGESTED AFFIRMATIONS

The way I have lived has brought no lasting satisfaction.
There is a way that lifts and completes me. I now choose that way.

Through all my life I have known
There is something special for me to do.
I am ready to listen to my inner voice
And get on with my real purpose.

I am no longer pushed or pulled by conflicting motivations;
The way opens before me and I move confidently on my path.

When I act from the calm of my inner center
There is no room for uncertainty or conflict.

As I resolve inner conflicts,
I hear the clear, still whisper
Of Spirit and express peace.

There are two forces in this world,
One taking me Godward, the other delusionward.
I have the gift of free will;
I choose to use my treasure for that which endures.

Guilt

SOUL PERFECTION

The soul is made in the Image of God and so is perfect. It yearns to realize its natural state of oneness with God and His manifesting qualities. Intuitively we know this and want to work toward this inner perfection in our lives. An artist may strive to create a perfect masterpiece, a musician a perfect song. A businessman tries to create the ideal company and a wife the perfect home. We can move toward our goal as long as our attitudes and motivation are positive.

Sometimes this great desire can cause friction. We may expect perfection from a wife, a loved one, or an employee and put unreasonable demands on them. We may demand unrelenting perfection of ourselves and see each mistake as unforgivable. These unrealistic demands on ourselves and others result in deep-rooted guilt feelings and remorse.

This world is imperfect, and we are bound to make mistakes as things fluctuate and change. If the world had been created perfect, then no one would need to strive to evolve Godward. We can adopt a joyous attitude and strive to do our best in everything, knowing that we learn by our mistakes. We can leave results in God's hands and get on with our growth. If we bring in frustration and guilt because we have not been perfect, then we are adding negatives to something positive. If we view mistakes as guidelines to show us we are off the mark, we turn them into positives.

When you become aware that you are doing something against your highest good, be thankful for the insight. There is no need to hold onto the mistake or chastise yourselves with guilt feelings. Some people use guilt as a form of punishment. They seem to punish themselves as if that would make an action all right or prevent them from making another mistake. No amount of guilt can change the past. An honest mistake is not a sin, and guilt serves us only when it shows us we have not acted in our best interest. Then it needs to be dismissed and the energy released for constructive purposes.

We have been programmed to burn with shame, and many cannot stand their guilt feelings. They seek an outer stimulus to shake off their inner turmoil. They may take a drink or overeat. Guilt can be turned into a means of growth by analyzing what you did or did not do that brought undesirable results and making up your mind to profit from the learning, and then letting the situation go.

Remember that everyone makes mistakes in an imperfect world. When we unconsciously demand perfection in everything, we are setting ourselves up to fail and feel miserable. Keep in mind that many so-called mistakes result from unreasonable demands placed upon us by others which we tried to fulfill against impossible odds. We need to reflect and be realistic about what we consent to do for others. We may be taking away their opportunities to grow and setting ourselves up for feeling guilty no matter what we do.

The Heavenly Father is not concerned with our mistakes. He created us and understands our imperfect human nature. What stings the heart of God is our lack of love for ourselves and our indifference towards Him. If we learn to appreciate and love ourselves as God's children and do what is best for our own growth, then we shall be able to extend a hand to a brother or sister in need without trying to force our own conception of "Good" upon him or her. Remember, God does not judge you, and so it is unfair to place mistakes and guilt feelings between your Creator and yourself. Love Him as He loves you—unconditionally.

Chart Study: Guilt

If remorse or guilt is clouding your heart, then realistically look at the underlying causes and your own response to the situation. There are Creative Thought Remedies for your guilt feelings.

GUILT

Making a mistake is doing something that is not in your best interest.

Many mistakes we feel we have made are not mistakes at all but the limiting beliefs of a misinformed society.

↓

Examine the beliefs that you or society has imposed on you and see if they are really valid. Many are not.

↓

Many of the *shoulds* and *don'ts* that you got from parents you have already laid aside. When anything makes you uneasy, take time to analyze why and look at the belief behind it to see if it makes sense for you now.

↓

Realize that religions tend to be expert at producing guilt feelings for their own ends, which have nothing to do with the original teaching of the Master.

↓

Once you have learned from mistakes, dismiss feelings of guilt and change your beliefs so that they do not demand impossible things of you.

Many people hold on to guilt as a means of purifying themselves.

↓

They feel that if they punish themselves with guilt long enough and intensely enough it will overcome their mistakes.

↓

No amount of feeling guilty over something can change the past.

↓

Remember that what you focus on is what you experience and attract.

↓

The life-promoting way is to change our beliefs and thus our actions and so learn to live joyously and productively in the present moment of time, letting the past go.

↓

People who make a mistake often cannot stand feeling their remorse and so suppress it.

↓

Instead of looking at an unrealistic belief that they must be perfect or else remorseful, they plunge themselves into outer activity in order to shake off these feelings.

↓

Very often they then go back and make the same mistake again because they have not dealt with the underlying cause.

↓

God is not concerned with our mistakes. He looks at our motives and our desire to grow into the perfect pattern of our souls.

If your inner guidance lets you know that you have done something that prevents your growth, then give thanks and tell it it has served its purpose well.

↓

Having realized that your actions have not helped you live joyously and creatively, see how to change, and then get on with living more in accord with what does bring fulfillment and growth.

↓

Offer up your errors to God in the sanctuary of your Inner Self as mistakes only, knowing He understands and forgives all, for God is Love. It is not He who judges us. We mercilessly judge ourselves.

SUGGESTED AFFIRMATIONS

>By the law of Grace, I am forgiven.
>
>I forgive myself and others for past mistakes.
>
>Past mistakes and deeds serve as learning experiences;
>I move on and leave the past behind.
>
>I accept what I've done and ask to be guided
>According to my highest good.
>
>I answer only to myself and my Creator;
>I give up trying to be all the things others expect.
>
>I am striving to do my best;
>Sometimes I win, sometimes I lose:
>I learn from my failures and let them go,
>For I am always growing and doing better.
>
>My soul is clear and perfect;
>Mistakes can never tarnish it.
>I patiently and gently work to manifest
>The innate perfection of my soul.

Inner Voices on Food

For most people, eating is a required function of living. The average person living for 70 years with three meals a day partakes of 76,650 acts of eating in a lifetime. Even if we are young, we can see the many habit patterns we have built up around food. If one feels better from exercising daily and eating healthful food, one will continue this practice. If a person cannot stand the thought of living without coffee, for example, he or she will likely continue to crave it.

In theory the digestive process is very simple. Food is acquired, chewed in the mouth, digested in the stomach and intestine, and absorbed into the bloodstream to feed the cells. Waste products are then excreted. However, the practice of eating is far more complex because of programmed attitudes about the desire or need for food and the enjoyment we have connected to eating it. Some are indifferent and eat out of necessity, others are attached to the pleasure of eating and find it a necessity.

DIET AND ATTITUDES

If we wish to diet, the first sensible step is to explore attitudes toward food. Food alone has little meaning until thought is applied to it. Subconscious memories, conceptions, and experiences with eating will determine how one approaches a meal. If one wishes to diet, then he or she needs to look at his emotional patterns and beliefs about food. These will make or break an ability to stick to a diet. Too often our beliefs about ourselves and our emotions and feelings are what undo us when we wish to change our eating patterns.

One of the stumbling blocks may be a tendency to pay little attention to what we are eating and just cram it in, chew it a little, and swallow it. If we can change this whole process or habit, we can move a long way down the road to being in charge of our eating patterns.

Simple, thoughtfully prepared dishes made with loving attention are imbued with special properties. Making the setting attractive and

blessing the food before we begin focus attention on what the food is for.

If the eating is done slowly, savouring the flavours and enjoying them while we thoroughly chew them, we shall find we are satisfied with far less than if we thoughtlessly bolted what was on our plate or washed it down with liquid.

Most important is never to eat when you are upset, angry, frustrated, or worried. If necessary, go for a run or a brisk walk or punch a pillow or otherwise work off the negative feelings in a physical way so that you can sit down calmly and appreciate and enjoy what is before you. Negative feelings upset the system, spoil the digestion, and turn foods into toxic waste in the system.

CHART STUDY: INNER VOICES ON FOOD

If we wish to diet or overcome unnatural food cravings, it will help if we study the attitudes of the conscious mind. You may find that many of the limiting thoughts expressed in the following chart are the very ones that play havoc in your dieting. The Creative Thought Remedies give you alternatives. The affirmations can help you move to where you want to be.

INNER VOICES ON FOOD

Destructive Practices

Early conditioning that connected food with love or comfort.

Using Food for Stimulation
↓

Inner Whispers of a False Reasoning in the Conscious Mind

Eat quickly so I can be first to get seconds.

I can shove in a little more, I do not feel stuffed yet.

It's a bother to chew my food, so I will wash it down with water.

I will indulge today and cut down tomorrow.

I'll start my diet tomorrow.

Never mind yesterday's indigestion and resolution, why not eat the tasty fried food?

Eat, drink, and be merry; who cares about tomorrow?

Eat all you can, you can always use a laxative.
↓

Results

These attitudes lead to overweight, constipation, heart problems, arthritis, suffering.

Once the bodily temple is damaged, it takes a great deal of self-denial to bring it back to health.

Unhappiness, poor health, pain, and premature death come from this mistreatment of our bodies.

Enhancing Our Total Selves

Memories of the joy of well-being and good health.

Wholesome Food
↓

Intelligent Reasoning of the Conscious Mind

I eat nourishing foods to maintain my body temple, which is my vehicle of expression while in this world.

Little food is necessary when I tap into the Energy of Spirit.

Certain foods produce calmness and health and leave me relaxed and tranquil.

Pure, natural foods keep my body free from toxins and stress and let me feel alert and wonderful.

Food is for nourishing the body, not the senses. I will eat only when I am really hungry.

My teeth were given me to chew my food. My stomach is for digestion.

Others are starving in this world; why should I overeat?
↓

Results

Eating wisely brings me health and happiness.

When my body is strong and well, I enjoy living in it.

I can make my body a fit temple for my soul to aid in my growth.

Suggested Affirmations

Food is a means to an end,
Not an end in itself.
I eat to keep my body temple
Healthy and whole.

When I am angry, frustrated, or resentful
I turn to a physical activity
To work off the feeling, instead of eating.

When I am lonesome or feeling low
I call up a friend and talk instead of seeking solace in food.

When I bless my food and eat it slowly
I really enjoy it and never overeat.

I treat my body as the temple of the Holy Spirit;
I nourish it wisely and show it respect.

Food nourishes my body; love nourishes all the rest of me.

I choose life-giving food to nourish me.

I chew my food thoroughly and slowly.

I am substantial the way I am; I no longer need to stuff myself.

As I let go of my burdens, excess flesh melts away.

My greater self exists without food;
I eat only to nourish my body.
I pray and meditate
To nourish my Greater Self.

The Healing Crisis

The Healing Process

The art of healing begins with the removal of beliefs, attitudes, and practices that result in pain and suffering in body, mind, heart, or soul. When inharmonies are removed, then consciousness can shine out in its native inner beauty and heal and make us whole.

Physical healing begins with commonsense change to better health habits. The requirements include a wholesome diet, daily exercise, bodily cleanliness, sufficient rest, and periodic physical assessment. Health can be maintained only by keeping the body free from tension and the buildup of toxic materials. When this is accomplished the inner energies flow smoothly, maintaining bodily functions in a state of glowing health.

Mental healing begins with the removal of limiting thoughts from the mind so that it can be charged with healing wisdom. Emotional healing is brought about by understanding and dealing with disturbing feelings so that we can feel calmness, love, peace, and joy within. Spiritual healing comes from realization of our own worth as a unique child of God and of the soul's oneness with Spirit.

The Healing Crisis

During the process of healing there usually are crisis points on the journey to wholeness. When we work with natural remedies, affirmations, and meditation techniques we shall experience the effects of the removal of layers of toxicity, limiting mental programming, emotional disharmonies, and soul suppression. We may see glimpses of soul qualities, but these will tend to be overshadowed by the reawakening of emotional dramas and negative experiences buried in the subconscious mind. The mixture of expanding and limiting qualities emerging into our awareness can cause a state of confusion or of upset and alarm.

When physical healing is taking place toxins that have been held in the body begin to be released through the bloodstream to be excreted. Often they make one feel terrible as the body reacts to them on their way out. We are so used to instant pain relief and instant cures

(that only suppress the underlying cause) that we feel something is wrong and may shut down the body's attempt to rid itself of waste.

If we can be patient, trust the body's wisdom and see it through then the healing can take place, and a wonderful sense of well-being will eventually follow. We need to remember that it has taken a long time for the body to get so choked and clogged with waste, and so we must give it time to cleanse, even though we may be uncomfortable in the process.

This getting worse before we can feel better is called the *healing crisis*.

During the mental and emotional and spiritual healing crisis we need to encourage ourselves to introspect and watch the flow of thoughts and emotions. When a disquieting memory or feeling arises, spend time determining the root cause. If you can address it with calmness and let the soul's wisdom work, you can recall what caused the disruptive thing and understand and concentrate on rectifying the situation, if need be, or just replacing it with positive feedback.

CHART STUDY: THE HEALING CRISIS

If you are experiencing a healing crisis, it may help to study the following chart and understand the transformation process.

THE HEALING CRISIS

Negative thoughts, feelings, and actions coupled with a toxic body are the main causes of mankind's maladies.

↓

Meditation techniques, positive affirmations, natural and holistic practices and therapies can help to heal.

↓

Toxins can be removed from my consciousness as well as from my body.

↓ ↓

Awakening of Buried Emotional Dramas and Negative Tendencies

Awakening of Inner Awareness

Emotions from the subconscious mind such as feelings of inferiority or injustice, fears, resentments, grief, etc., will tend to surface.

Opening to the superconscious mind, experiencing inner qualities of the soul, and knowing our own uniqueness and capacity to love and be loved.

↓

Overwhelming Emotions

Various emotions and divine realizations bubble up to the conscious mind and may cause real confusion in the beginning.

↓

Introspection (Self-Analysis)

Watch the thoughts and feelings that arise and ask yourself: Where do they come from? How did I acquire them? What is the cause of them? What are they doing to me? How can I develop the constructive tendencies and transmute the destructive or limiting ones?

↓

Inner Healing

It is necessary to notice and deal with any trauma, guilt, resentment, or other negativities that emerge. This will free up energy for joyous living and for developing your soul qualities and bringing them into your everyday life.

SUGGESTED AFFIRMATIONS

I have the courage and the strength to transform myself.

As I allow painful memories to surface,
I know they are being released and healed.

As I cooperate with my body, I have patience and faith
That my inner wisdom is bringing me health and well-being.

When indecision and doubts assail me
I return to my sense of inner trust and am healed.

I am healed, balanced, harmonized, and attuned
Physically, emotionally, mentally, and spiritually.

Every cell of my body is charged by the Light of God.
Every fiber of my being is bathed in the Radiance of God.
I am whole and well, for God's Healing Light is what I am.

I am made from the Light of God.
This Radiance cannot be destroyed.
God's Light within me is perfect and whole.
I am immortal, radiant, and whole.

Part Six

PERSONALIZED THOUGHT REMEDY CHART

A Master Is One Who Listens.

Making and Using a Personal Chart

Working through the various charts in our text will have helped you develop skills in understanding your own response patterns. The exercises are intended to enhance your clarity and help you become aware of the direction of your own innate tendencies. They can help you be more prosperous and inspire you in your development. By understanding and acknowledging our less desirable traits, we can replace them with life-promoting ones.

Making the Chart

Let us now make a Personalized Thought Remedy Chart. This method is designed to help discover where our shortcomings are and give us more awareness of our God-given talents and attributes. The method is simple but can be most helpful and transforming. We need to supply sincerity and effort.

1. The first step is to draw a good-sized circle in the middle of a large piece of blank paper. A circle is a symbol for a whole, and it represents your Inner Self or Soul. Write inside the circle a positive quality you wish to manifest.

As children of God, we do not have to acquire anything from outside; all divine qualities are within us waiting to be rediscovered so that they may shine forth. By placing a quality inside the circle, you remind your consciousness of the new centre from which you now wish to operate. The quality could be love, joy, peace, calmness, kindness, a mantra, a prayer—anything that you wish to manifest. In our example we have chosen the attribute of joy.

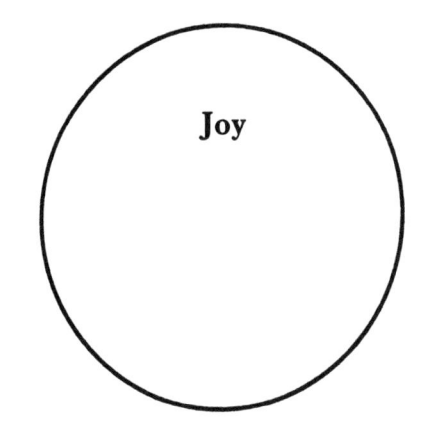

If you find at this point in your life that a negative quality is so overpowering that you cannot concentrate on a positive one, then proceed to Step Three.

2. If an inspirational thought or realization comes to you that helps ground you in your centre of joy or whatever quality you have chosen, make a check mark inside your circle and write it down. If the realization that inner joy is your divine birthright helps you to become more firmly established in joy, then write it down. You may think of many things to write down now or you may find others coming to mind from time to time. Be sure to keep track of them when they come to you.

Joy

✓ As a child of God, inner joy is my divine birthright.

3. Be aware of all the factors that tend to take you away from your centre of joy, be it from memory or imagination, or from your interactions with people and situations. Perhaps you become aware of a feeling of sadness or despondency. You are not quite sure how this feeling came about and took hold of you. In order to understand and let go of this, write it down outside your circle.

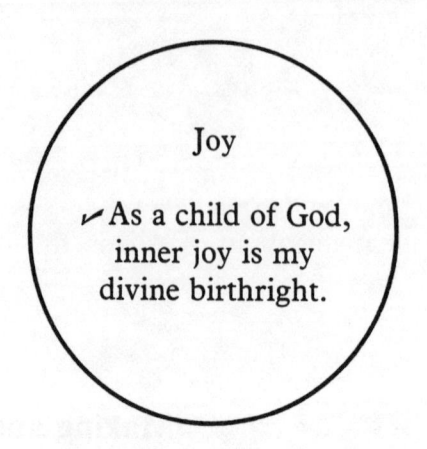

Joy

✓ As a child of God, inner joy is my divine birthright.

X Sorrow and Despondency

4. Gently but steadily observe your thoughts and interactions with others. You will probably discover that whenever you think of your faults or hear someone mention them, a feeling of uneasiness, guilt, or hopelessness descends on you. Record this realization in writing outside your circle.

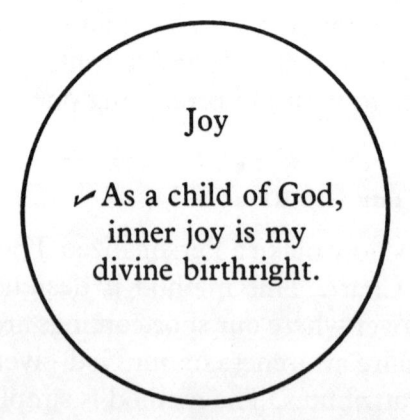

Joy

✓ As a child of God, inner joy is my divine birthright.

X Sorrow and Despondency
X Sadness or uneasiness manifests whenever I think of, or hear someone mention, my faults or failings.

5. The next step is to place a positive thought or experience inside your circle to help you move away from the tendency to feel sadness or uneasiness from criticism by others or from your own awareness of the things you feel inadequate about. Perhaps the understanding that this world is an imperfect place and that we are here to do our best and leave the results in God's hands will help to lift your spirits again. Whatever helps should also be written down and repeated till it is fixed firmly in your mind and attitudes.

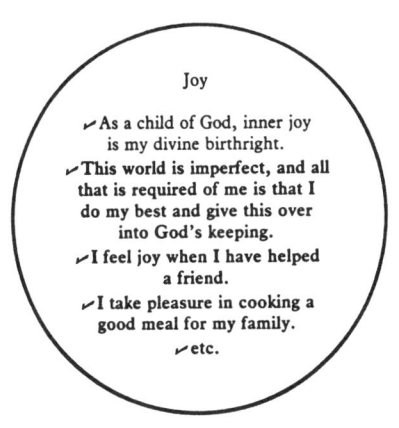

> Joy
> ✓ As a child of God, inner joy is my divine birthright.
> ✓ This world is imperfect, and all that is required of me is that I do my best and give this over into God's keeping.
> ✓ I feel joy when I have helped a friend.
> ✓ I take pleasure in cooking a good meal for my family.
> ✓ etc.

X Sorrow and Despondency
X Sadness or uneasiness manifests whenever I think of, or hear someone mention, my faults or failings.

6. Continue the process and work with it daily, adding insights until you are firmly established in the soul quality you have decided to manifest. Remember that we have all been told over and over of our weaknesses or faults and rarely praised for our good qualities. Now is the time to list your strengths and claim them. Are you capable of giving compassion and love? Do you support your friends? What are the things you do well?

SUGGESTIONS AND INSPIRATION

1. It is best to make one large Thought Remedy Chart as your main draft and carry a small notebook along with you to record daily happenings. At the end of each day place your check marks and *X*s for new insights on your main draft and reflect upon them. Go over the positive ones and give yourself credit.

2. Study your chart as an impartial observer, detaching yourself so that you are not discouraged or alarmed at the life-diminishing habits that you see. When we keep our consciousness revolving around the positive thoughts and actions that we have placed inside our circle, it becomes easier to see that our strengths more than balance out our weaknesses.

Because we have been conditioned to focus on our shortcomings, it is often hard to call to mind our strengths. Take time; reflect on the positive qualities you do have. Ask friends or co-workers to tell you things they like about you. Acknowledge them and put them in your circle. The idea is to claim even seemingly minor strengths so that you finally come to see that your strengths do outweigh the shortcomings, and this will help you become firmly established in your centre through the realization

that the real you is strong and beautiful in God's sight.

3. Try this for a week and then see if you discover any patterns from the *X*s. Draw a flow diagram of your reactions and all the various facets of it. See if you can determine the underlying causes of any negative tendencies you uncover.

If you find you are fearful, reflect on what you are fearful of and give it a label. Then place the opposite quality inside your circle. Instead of rejecting the fear and suppressing it, look into it and experience it. Just let it flow so that it spends itself. Notice and even record step by step the various reactions you feel when experiencing it. Find out which belief is the basis of this fear in the present circumstances and see if it is a valid one. Usually we will find it is not. If, for example, you shake with fear when you enter a doctor's office, find out if the reason for this is a fear of authority figures, or of disease, or of pain or death, or that some fault or weakness in you might be exposed. Go through your reactions from beginning to end and record them in sequential order. It can be profitable to do this. You may discover that the fear was valid when you were a child but is groundless now, and you can let it go.

Watch other situations in your life when fear comes up and see if it relates to this experience. If you see that it does relate, then label the fear and map it out from the stimulus situation through your reactions and take a long look at the belief that brought it on. Our fears are usually based on fear of disapproval, because approval was so vitally important to us as children. When we really examine it with adult eyes we see that we need give it no power now. When you find it has no relevance now, you can put the new belief about yourself into your circle. If you do this faithfully for several weeks, you will be amazed how much you will learn about yourself. Keep adding to your chart and revising it, and you can gradually see your life patterns. When they are no longer hidden, you will be able to take charge of them and manifest what you want in your life instead.

4. The secret of this method is to bring your negative patterns to your awareness so you can now deal with them. The unknown is usually what we fear. Once something is known, we can deal with it. By continuous watchfulness, effort, and by sticking to your new discipline, you can begin to transform your negative patterns. To deny them and pretend they do not exist only drives them underground and gives them power over us. When emotions are bottled up within us they will eventually explode and carry us away. We can take back power over our own patterns of behaviour so that we can act instead of reacting. In this way we can work with them and transmute them. This is done by keeping your main concentration on the quality you want to cultivate and on the check marks you have placed inside the circle. Your consciousness responds to what you focus on, so keep it revolving around the positive inspirations and realizations that have come to you.

5. When your Thought Remedy Chart is finished, memorize it. When something triggers a reaction in you, use your power of recall to bring back a mental picture of the patterns you discovered. You will soon come to recognize these patterns as soon as they are triggered and will be able to short-circuit the reaction and turn it to the quality you wish to

cultivate. Soon you will be able to deal with any situation that arises.

Very often when an insight comes we shortly forget it. By working with your Thought Remedy Chart persistently, you can have instantaneous recall of what you have learned and so can put it to use.

6. As you continue to use your chart, your own centre of being will become stronger and stronger, and your negative, destructive tendencies will begin to fall away. When you feel firmly rooted in your centre with your chosen quality and feel that it is a firmly established part of your being, you are ready to try another quality. In this way you can gradually become master of yourself. Do not be discouraged if you notice that you fall back into old patterns now and then. Just keep working, for it takes time to release old conditioning. As you have more and more success, the relapses will come less and less frequently and you will find you can abort them before they can begin to take you over.

Remember, too, that saints were not made overnight—a lot of effort, attention, and purification went into the process. If you keep on working even after setbacks, you are already victorious, for God knows your heart. If your motives are good, you already have His blessing, and in His eyes you are already succeeding. God truly does help those who help themselves. Persistence in your efforts will bring help without fail.

7. If you wish to understand your relationship with someone else, draw two circles—one for each of you—and write down your ✓s and Xs in your own along with the other person's responses. Do not presume to make a chart for them. We never truly know another person. We only carry our own ideas of who and what he or she is. All you can do is see what response your interaction brings. By changing what you do and watching the other's response you will learn how to make this relationship work better. You will soon learn how you communicate with each other and what areas need working on. If two people wish to work on this together, it brings an added benefit to both in discovering more about their relationship and helps to break down problems and enhance communication and so throw new light on any difficulties that exist. Remember, though, that we can change only ourselves—but when *we* change, it changes others around us, because we now act differently, and they have to respond to us in a different way.

8. The following Thought Remedy Charts are complete and condensed observations of typical people. They are the result of the building of many Thought Remedy Charts in which the tendencies were recorded and crystalized. These charts are offered as examples only, since your Thought Remedy Chart will be quite different because it will be your own, and you are unique.

Feelings of Unworthiness

↓

X Feelings of being unloved and unworthy of love from childhood.

↓

X Since I feel unloved, I have a great need to be loved.

↓

X In all relationships in life I try to get others to love me to prove that I am lovable.

↓

X I constantly do things to get my mate to prove that he/she loves me. I am never satisfied by anything he/she does or says because I feel unworthy of love.

↓

X I interpret our interactions in a way to further a belief that he/she loves me for what I do rather than who I am.

↓

X The result is a greater feeling of loneliness and unworthiness and an impossible situation for him/her.

↓

X This is forcing him/her to come to the very point I fear—giving up on our relationship.

PERSONALIZED THOUGHT REMEDY CHART

Self-Love
- ✓ I am loved by Love itself, which is God, and that Love is within me. It is my birthright.
- ✓ God has created me as a beautiful, unique person. There is no other like me, and He loves me as I am.
- ✓ As I focus on love, negative emotions lose their hold on me.
- ✓ I have decided to speak and act out of love instead of fear.

✓ I examine my strengths and do not dwell on my weaknesses.

✓ Expressing love means caring enough to be honest about my own worth and expressing my positive feelings toward others.

✓ As I give love and approval to others, it comes back to me.

Fear of Rejection

↓

X I find it difficult to take the risk of expressing myself openly and honestly.

↓

X I feel that if my mate gets too close to me and finds out what I am like, he/she will not love me.

↓

X I fear and so avoid sharing my inner thoughts and feelings, and this stops us from having an intimate relationship.

↓

X I find it very difficult to realize that a fault I see in my mate is one I also carry, or to be willing to admit my own mistakes to him/her.

↓

X Whenever my mate confronts me with my faults or mistakes I withdraw in fear and react with anger and scorn. This makes a bad scene, which he/she does not like.

↓

X My mate becomes agitated when I do not communicate openly and honestly with him/her. Up till now I pretended this was his/her problem, not mine.

↓

X Knowing that my mate is upset causes me greater fear and insecurity.

↓

X I am afraid my mate will give up on our relationship and leave.

Suppression of Emotions

↓

X I have a fear of expressing inner emotions.

↓

X I suppress emotions and hide them.

↓

X I experience nightmares when I sleep as my mind is relaxed.

↓

X My feelings build within me like an overheated oven and then explode and fly at everyone around me.

↓

X This increases my anger at everything and everyone.

↓

X Then I feel anger and disquiet at myself for exploding and dumping my feelings on others, though I quickly rationalize this.

↓

X I make myself depressed but blame it on others.

↓

X I strive harder to suppress my anger, depression, and other emotions.

↓

X This starts the cycle all over again.

PERSONALIZED THOUGHT REMEDY CHART

Relax and Experience Life
- ✓ I will be gentle with myself.
- ✓ I'll kick a football instead of bottling up my emotions and putting a strain on my heart and family.
- ✓ Love and joy are better than tension and depression.
- ✓ Meditation is the art of loving God. In love there is no fear.

✓ I will relax and contact the finest that is in me without fear.

✓ I will examine what comes up when I meditate and deal with it instead of being afraid of it.

✓ I am taking time alone to feel my emotions and deal with them instead of suppressing them.

✓ I no longer explode.

✓ I find my children coming to me with their problems now and can help them.

Fear of the Unknown

↓

X I experience the fear of uncertainty and potential loss of control.

↓

X During meditation I experience tremendous fear when my heart slows down and my mind becomes still. I also fear what will surface.

↓

X My panic makes me more agitated than when I started to meditate.

↓

X I lose the peace that the meditation started to bring me.

↓

X I experience anger at myself for panicking.

↓

X I make myself depressed.

↓

X I feel like giving up the spiritual life entirely.

↓

Fear of Loss of Control

Fear of Failure

↓

X I fear that I will not be a good mother to my children, so I avoid the issue by pushing them away.

↓

X I fear that I will not get ahead in life and will miss out if I have to look after my children, so I don't pay attention when they want to talk to me about what seems unimportant to me.

↓

X I resent it that my children do not tell me things I think are important.

↓

X I take offence if my husband says anything that implies my housekeeping is not perfect. I am afraid of any criticism.

↓

X I notice that he is avoiding me as much as he can.

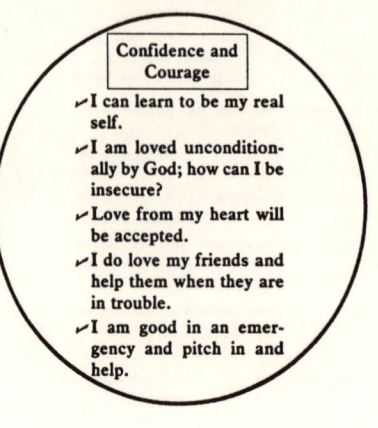

PERSONALIZED THOUGHT REMEDY CHART

Confidence and Courage

- ✓ I can learn to be my real self.
- ✓ I am loved unconditionally by God; how can I be insecure?
- ✓ Love from my heart will be accepted.
- ✓ I do love my friends and help them when they are in trouble.
- ✓ I am good in an emergency and pitch in and help.

✓ I forget myself and run to the aid of my children.

✓ I can get a good meal up for a group when I need to.

✓ I come fearlessly to the rescue of an animal I see being hurt or mistreated.

Insecurity (fear of rejection)

↓

X I try to create opportunities for myself in an underhanded manner and force my way into situations rather than being upfront and honest.

↓

X I tend to force my love and affection on others in order to overcome my insecurity and fear of rejection.

↓

X I try to hide my fear by acting superior to make myself look better than I am.

↓

X I try to convince everyone that I am spiritually superior and that God is working through me so that I get respect.

↓

X People turn away from me because they see that I am phony and pretend love to gain attention so I will not feel insecure.

↓

X When people see through my mask I put up my defenses and strike out.

↓

X I feel more insecure when people push me away, so I start the whole process over again.

PERSONALIZED THOUGHT REMEDY CHART

Fear of God

↓

X In church I constantly heard that we were sinners. This reinforced what my parents told me about myself.

↓

X Since I was convinced I was a sinner, I thought I was unworthy of God's love.

↓

X Since I got punishment for every bad thing I did, I got to feel I was a bad person and deserved to be punished.

↓

X Since I feel I deserve to be punished, I believe that God feels the same way about me.

↓

X Since God knows all things, He is aware of how bad I am and disapproves of me.

↓

X Thus I relate only to a punishing God and have a fear relationship with Him.

↓

X This kind of thinking makes me feel I deserve eternal punishment and that God will give it to me, so I am afraid of God and find it hard to love Him or believe He can love me.

Love of God

✓ God is love, not fear or punishment, and He loves me just as I am.

✓ God is not so much concerned about my mistakes as He is about the love I give Him, myself, and others.

✓ My soul is beautiful. Whatever mistakes I make are only part of learning and do not make me a bad person.

✓ **Everyone makes mistakes, even saints; so I need not feel bad about mine.**

✓ **Mistakes are a necessary part of learning. Only those who do nothing make no mistakes.**

✓ **Now that I feel all right about myself, I feel better about God.**

✓ **Loving and accepting myself, I do not need praise to make me feel all right, and I do not respond with hurt when someone else is critical.**

Inner Insecurity

↓

X My parents continually told me I was bad whenever I failed to fit into their image of what they wanted me to be.

↓

X Almost everything I did seemed to be a mistake, and mistakes were terrible things.

↓

X By continually hearing that I was bad and receiving very little praise for the things I did well, I believed that I was a terrible person.

↓

X I formed relationships with people who treated me the way my parents treated me because that was what I was used to and believed I deserved.

↓

X I expected my husband to be critical of me and punish me, and that is exactly what he does.

↓

X This reinforces my feelings of unworthiness and that I deserve punishment.

Cassette Tapes For Meditation and Relaxation
by Alex Jones

Instrumental Music

KALI'S DREAM   *Piano*

Joyful piano melodies ripple like cool mountain streams, and the moods change colors like the seasons. Alex Jones is well known as a New Age musician whose pure and crystal-clear solo piano compositions evoke a subtle and beautiful feeling that just isn't present in much popular music. The music expresses the creative play and the depth of Nature in a way that touches the peace and beauty within each listener.

AWAKE AND DREAMING   *Piano & Synthesizer*

Devotional in nature, these simple melodies soothe the aching of your soul with a mellow blend of piano and synthesizer. The nine cuts are like gentle lullabies that enfold you in loving peace. The softer side of electronic music, perfect after a tiring day.

LOKAS: SPHERES OF PEACE   *Piano*

Celestial piano melodies that are truly a feast for the ears and upliftment for the soul. Performed in a classical style, the ten selections flow gently and slowly and will align a stressed mind and body with its calming space. The soothing music will carry the listener on a transforming voyage of peace.

PRANAVA   *Flute & Harp*

The flute and harp selections interlace to create a musical tapestry that is tranquil and yet uplifting. All selections have a depth of devotion and peace that is unparalleled. The ten compositions are very quiet and gentle. Such is their sublime simplicity that the effect on the nervous system is one of instantaneous calm. The penetrating music truly brings one's essence into balance and harmony.

INSIDE THE HOLLOW   *Piano & Synthesizer*

By popular request we are making available as a solo instrumental cassette the background music from *Infinite Directions*. From Side 1 you will feel the expansive music of the piano and synthesizer awaken unexplored realms of inner consciousness. Side 2 is devotional in nature, and the piano and synthesizer move the heart to the gentleness of love.

Guided Meditations

ANGELS OF COLOR & SOUND   *Guided Meditation (Narration) with Piano Background*

Angels of Color is a guided meditation on the seven rays emanating from the seven chakras or spinal centers in the body. With this tape each chakra will be stimulated by listening to inspiring musical selections and narration that are in resonance with each chakra. By following the guided color meditation, the seven rays of divine qualities, vitality, courage, joy, love, peace, intuition, and soul realization will be awakened.

Angels of Sound is solo piano compositions that bring tranquility to a restless mind.

INFINITE DIRECTIONS   *Guided Meditation (Narration) with Piano Background*

Two guided meditations. Side 1 is a visualization exercise to help one feel an expansion of consciousness. The mind's true nature is Cosmic Consciousness and is not limited to the conscious or subconscious state. With the aid of this visualization one can sense that one is the infinite, omnipresent, limitless soul.

Side 2 is a meditation on self-love and confidence. Through this visualization exercise one can begin to feel a connection with the Creator and understand that one is a child of God. Re-identification with the beauty within opens the door to all positive expressions and the growth of confidence and self-respect.

IMAGINATION'S DOOR   *Affirmations (Narration) with Piano Background*

Affirmations work on the principle of magnetism. When revolving our will-power around a thought, a force field is set up drawing within its circle that which is being affirmed. Through the proper use of affirmations in this cassette we can realize total health and our own divinity.

BOOKS AND CASSETTES AVAILABLE FROM:

in Canada

Eastern Gate Publishing Inc.
Att/Alex Jones
23 Rivercourt Blvd.
Toronto, Ontario
Canada M4J 3A3

in U.S.A.

Eastern Gate Publishing (VA) Inc.
Att/Alex Jones
P.O. Box 1485
Front Royal, VA 22630

Also by Alex Jones

Seven Mansions of Color

This book offers inspirational and practical methods for the use of color in one's daily life. Color can aid each of us physically, mentally, emotionally, and spiritually. It works on definite scientific principles, and when we apply these laws we will experience harmony within ourselves and with others. **Seven Mansions of Color** will show you how to tap the inner potential of color so that you may enrich your life and become a radiant, full-spectrum person.

CONTENTS:

COLOR CREATION—A study of the creation of vibrations of which the universe is made. Everything vibrates to various colors that influence our lives.

QUALITIES OF COLOR—An explanation of the various qualities of colors so that you may gain the power to choose harmonious colors to enhance your life.

COSMIC COLOR RAYS—Directions are given to enable you to work in harmony with the seven color rays emanating from the White Light of Spirit to bring about perfect health in body, mind, and spirit.

SPIRITUAL AWARENESS THROUGH COLOR—An in-depth study of the mystical experiences of saints and sages of many spiritual disciplines who attuned their consciousness to the Seven Cosmic Color Rays and manifested them in their lives.

COLOR IN THE AURA—Learn to interpret and strengthen the colors in your aura. When we purify the aura we live as true children of light.

COLOR MEDITATION—Study the art of color meditation so that you can saturate yourself with the qualities of vitality, courage, joy, love, peace, intuition, and soul realization.

HEALING PROPERTIES OF COLOR—An outline on the properties of color and their influence on the anatomy.

COLOR IN THE HOME AND WARDROBE—Discover the proper color concepts in home decor and dress so that you can permeate your environment with the best life has to offer. Surrounding yourself with harmonious colors uplifts and makes you positive and joyous.

COLOR IN INDUSTRY—Outlines the proper color schemes that can lower accident rates, decrease nervous tension and eye strain. Discover the colors that increase efficiency and morale and give various advantages in advertising.

OTHER TOPICS INCLUDED ARE: Radiant and pigment colors; the color essences of foods and other elements; color lamps; color and world cycles; color breathing; rejuvenation with color; color and art; and color and music.

160 pages   ISBN: 0-87516-500-1   A DeVorss Publication